# MORE PLAYS

MACMILLAN AND CO., Limited
LONDON · BOMBAY · CALCUTTA · MADRAS
MELBOURNE

THE MACMILLAN COMPANY
NEW YORK · BOSTON · CHICAGO
DALLAS · ATLANTA · SAN FRANCISCO

THE MACMILLAN COMPANY
OF CANADA, LIMITED
TORONTO

# MORE PLAYS

*by*

## LENNOX ROBINSON

NEW YORK
THE MACMILLAN COMPANY
1935

PRINTED IN GREAT BRITAIN

# CONTENTS

# ALL'S OVER, THEN?

## A PLAY IN THREE ACTS

The first production of *All's Over, Then?* took place on July 25, 1932, in the Abbey Theatre, Dublin, with the following cast:

| | | |
|---|---|---|
| MAGGIE . . . . . . | | Shelah Richards |
| HENRY . . . . . . | | Barry Fitzgerald |
| JULIA . . . . . . | | Ria Mooney |
| ELEANORE . . . . . | | Eileen Crowe |
| DOCTOR BOESON . . . . | | F. J. McCormick |
| ARTHUR . . . . . . | | Arthur Shields |

The play was produced by the Author.

## CHARACTERS

(In the Order of their Appearance)

MAGGIE.
HENRY.
JULIA.
ELEANORE.
DR. BOESON.
ARTHUR.

The First and Third Acts take place in the sitting-room of the Swinnerton's flat, the Second Act takes place in Maggie's room. No time elapses between the First and Second Acts—in fact they slightly overlap; the Third Act takes place the morning after the Second Act.

# ACT I

SCENE: *A sitting-room. Obviously the room of intelligent, cultured people. Notably in the room a grand or semi-grand piano. A small gramophone somewhere, a telephone and the necessary tables and chairs. There are no windows visible, for there is a door on the left and a door centre, and the right side is filled by a fireplace. The pictures on the walls—and there are many of them—may be prints or originals of French pictures of the impressionist period or perhaps very good reproductions of great, but not hackneyed, masterpieces of Italy and Spain. There is, at any rate, no hint of modernity about the room nor is it, on the other hand, Victorian or ninetyish, it seems the cultivated taste of 1900 or a little later. It must be evening, for the electric light is lit and there is a brightly burning fire.*

*The door on the left opens and a charming girl comes into the room. She is aged twenty, her name is* MAGGIE. *She is dressed in a very pretty, fashionable evening dress. She is followed by a man who looks about forty years old;*

5

*he is not in evening dress, just in a dark suit.*
*The man's name is* HENRY. MAGGIE *crosses at*
*once to the fire.*

MAGGIE. Oh, the fire's nice, the dining-room
was beastly cold.

HENRY. Yes, those gas-fires are no use. If
you're close to them, you're roasted; if you're five
feet from them, you freeze.

MAGGIE. And I was the other side of the
table from it. . . . I thought Eleanore was
coming, I thought she was just behind us.

HENRY (*sits on sofa*). She stayed to look after
something—lock up the biscuits or the claret.
. . . I say, what a stunning dress. I didn't
notice it at dinner.

MAGGIE. Naturally you didn't; you couldn't.
Most of it was under the table. What time
is it?

HENRY (*looking at his watch*). Just eight.

MAGGIE. Arthur's not due till a quarter past.

HENRY. Will that give you time enough?

MAGGIE. Bags. The concert doesn't start
till a quarter to nine.

HENRY. These modern concerts! In my
time they started at eight—sometimes at a
quarter to.

MAGGIE. Imagine Angel Avila starting at
seven forty-five!

HENRY. I wonder have I ever heard him.

MAGGIE. I'm sure not, darling, he's much

6

too modern for you, but you should. There's no one can play modern music like Angel. His French, his Spanish and his jazz!

HENRY. I doubt whether Arthur will like him.

MAGGIE. I'm sure he won't, but he'll get a kick out of it; it will give him something to think about when he goes back to his awful little hill-station in India and starts again making roads and bridges.

HENRY. Nice chap.

MAGGIE. It's rotten luck that on his first leave for five years he should find himself tied hand and foot to that odious old chief of his— that old stupid who changes his mind every two minutes.

HENRY. Well, he'll be gone to-morrow——the old stupid, I mean.

MAGGIE. Thank goodness.

(*A* MAID *enters with a tray of coffee, liqueurs and a few letters.*)

MAGGIE. Put it there, will you, Julia. . . . Thanks.

(*The* MAID *goes out.* MAGGIE *pours coffee for* HENRY *and for herself.*)

MAGGIE. A liqueur?

HENRY. A cognac, I think.

(*She pours it, gives it to him and his coffee.*)

HENRY. Liqueur for you?

MAGGIE. No thanks. (*She looks through the letters.*) Nothing for you, Henry, two circulars

7

for Eleanore, press-cuttings for me.    (*She starts to open them.*)

HENRY. Nice ones, I hope.

MAGGIE. Oh listen: the *Victuallers' Gazette* says: "Miss Maggie Swinnerton shows a knowledge of life rare in this age of hasty generalisations. The French Riviera glows through her pages, the cicala thrums, the cypress blooms" —what nonsense, I suppose the idiot means mimosa. (*She throws down the cutting and looks at another.*) The *Cork Examiner* declares: "This is a serious indictment of life in the South of France. If the things in this book be true, we can only be too thankful that there is still a haven where pure young girls can——" oh rot! (*She tries another cutting.*) "Smart and very, very young. An innuendo in every sentence." There's *not*.

HENRY. Don't take those silly things too seriously.

MAGGIE. Darling, I don't. Let them be as stupid as they like, I have the laugh on them. This dress is my answer.

HENRY. I don't follow you for an instant.

MAGGIE. When you admired it, if I had been a really womanly woman I'd have said "That old rag? I've been wearing it for years." But as I'm not a w.-w. I admit that I bought it to-day; it's hot from the shop.

HENRY. And why?

MAGGIE. Because, darling, nice publishers

8

wrote to me and whispered, "twenty thousand".

HENRY. Twenty thousand!

MAGGIE. Twen-ty thou-sand! And no sign of the sales slackening, and all without the degradation of being recommended by some book society. Alone I done it. Isn't it rather overwhelming? But I was so uplifted I felt I had to do something rather splashy, so I went out and bought this perfectly swish dress.

HENRY. Darling, I'm so awfully glad.

MAGGIE. So am I. But it's a bit terrifying. Suppose my next novel is a complete flop.

HENRY. I don't believe for a moment it will be. Did you work much on it to-day.

MAGGIE. Not a line. I spent the whole day reading you—except when I buzzed out to buy the dress.

HENRY. And what did you think of me?

MAGGIE. I think it's very interesting.

HENRY. Oh, is that all?

MAGGIE. Look here, what about Eleanore's coffee. Don't you think I should put it near the fire to keep warm?

HENRY. Yes, good idea. Tepid coffee is so awful.

MAGGIE (*putting the pot on the hearth*). It won't boil, will it? That would be worse.

HENRY. I don't think so. . . . But what did you think of it really?

MAGGIE. It?

HENRY. Don't fence.    My book.

MAGGIE. You've made Scarlatti very interesting, you're beautifully documented, you've got those letters which no one has published before, you've discovered an opera no one knew existed; it *is* interesting but it lacks—well, it lacks weather.

HENRY. Weather?

MAGGIE. You know the thing I mean. "There was a certain day in March (or April or June) when the sirocco blew up hard from the south" . . . or "There came a day when the sun beat down pitilessly on the dusty eucalyptus trees and a young man tossed on a bed while the flies buzzed and banged themselves against the white walls of his room." Oh, you know.    That kind of thing has been overdone, but there is something to be said for getting the tang of the places Scarlatti lived in; and your biography hasn't just that particular tang.    And he lived in such colourful places. I've been at Trapani—at least I've hung round it for an hour in a steamer while motor-boats skeeted all round us—and it looked charming, full of character.    If you could stay there for a week, be in Naples for a fortnight, it would make all the difference, it would give the book life and colour.

HENRY. You think it's colourless?    Yes, perhaps it is.

MAGGIE. Not in the essentials, Henry, only

in the little things that don't really matter historically, and yet they do matter to the modern reader. It's because I think your book so awfully good—makes my silly little novel seem like tripe—that I want it to be that little bit better which will make all the difference. And you can get it better if you'll go and see those places and come back with a notebook stuffed with that pretty awful thing called "local colour".

HENRY. Poor Eleanore can't travel. She not only gets sea-sick, she gets train-sick.

MAGGIE. I remember. That time you came to see me three years ago at St. Raphael she was ill all the time. But why take Eleanore? Go alone.

HENRY. Alone?

MAGGIE. Or, if you're scared of going alone, take me. I speak French and Italian like a native—queer if I didn't, seeing I've been in those parts solidly for eight years. Why shouldn't we go together?

HENRY. Oh. . . . That would be fun, wouldn't it?

MAGGIE. The best of fun. I'd see you had a gorgeous time.

HENRY. I'm a little tired of — here. I haven't been abroad for three years, not since that time at St. Raphael.

(ELEANORE *comes in. She is a beautiful woman, looking fifty-five or maybe older.*

II B

*There is something a little strained in her manner. She is beautifully, very quietly, dressed, probably in black or grey.)*

MAGGIE. Eleanore, what has kept you? I put your coffee here to keep hot. *(She gets the coffee and pours her a cup.)*

ELEANORE. I was busy, I had little things to do. *(Seeing the circulars.)* Are these for me?

MAGGIE. Only circulars, I'm afraid.

ELEANORE. I adore circulars, they needn't be answered. *(She tears them across without looking at them.)* Thanks, darling. *(Taking the cup from* MAGGIE.) I thought you'd be gone to your concert.

MAGGIE. Plenty of time. Arthur's to call for me, you know.

ELEANORE. And afterwards you're going dancing, aren't you?

MAGGIE. Yes, Arthur's going to do me proud. Poor dear, he has so little time left before India and dullness and coolies.

ELEANORE. He'll enjoy the dancing. He dances beautifully, doesn't he? I'm afraid he may not enjoy—what's the pianist's name?

MAGGIE. Angel Avila.

ELEANORE. I don't believe in that name. It's a crib from Segovia.

MAGGIE. I don't believe in it either. But people—men—really *are* called Angel in Spain, and anyway he plays divinely.

ELEANORE. I've never heard him; I don't feel as if I want to.

MAGGIE. Darling, you stopped at Debussy and I think you consider even him a little shockingly modern.   But I'm educating Henry and when I've done with him I'll take you in hand.   Why Henry even likes this. (*She switches on the gramophone, a record is already on it; it is modern, very modern, American jazz. After twenty seconds, seeing that* ELEANORE *is suffering acutely, she switches it off.*)   You hate that, Eleanore?   You don't see anything in it?

ELEANORE. I feel like the old lady and the bagpipes;  she thanked God there wasn't a smell with them.

HENRY. It is hateful in a way, Eleanore, but there's something, a wonderful rhythm anyway.

ELEANORE. There was that man—I never can remember his name—who played Ravel and Debussy and de Falla, and then finished up by playing some little thing by Haydn—you remember, Henry?—it was like a cup of clear water after a lot of cocktails and sticky liqueurs.

HENRY. I remember.   Lovely, lovely.

(*The telephone rings.*)

ELEANORE. Answer it, Maggie, please.

MAGGIE (*at the phone*). Hallo. . . .   Yes, this is Miss Swinnerton speaking. . . .   Oh, Arthur, is that you?   I'm ready. . . .   You're not coming? . . .   Oh, what a pig, what an utter, utter swine. . . .   Of course I understand. . . .

No, of course it's not your fault and all is forgiven and forgotten; no, not quite forgiven for you must take me out some other night. . . . To-morrow? Yes, I can't pretend I'm engaged to-morrow night. . . . Dinner here at seven, and a theatre. . . . Right. . . . I'm so awfully sorry. Give the old geezer hell with my love. Good-bye. . . . Yes, all right. (*She rings off.*) Now isn't that the limit? He's been waiting in since half-past six for old Clarke to come along and now Clarke coolly phones that he can't come till half-past eight and that puts the lid on the concert as far as Arthur is concerned.

ELEANORE. Well, I think it's very thoughtless of Mr. Clarke.

HENRY. Arthur shouldn't stand for it.

MAGGIE. Darling, he has to. His future depends on keeping in Clarke's good books.

ELEANORE. Can't he join you later and take you dancing?

MAGGIE. He said nothing about it.

ELEANORE. Spoiling your evening like this.

MAGGIE. I don't mind the dancing, that happens any night. But to miss my beloved Avila!

ELEANORE. But you needn't lose Avila, darling. You have the tickets, go alone.

MAGGIE. I can't, not in this dress. I need support, someone to make me feel I'm all right.

ELEANORE. Couldn't you ring up someone?

MAGGIE. Too late.

ELEANORE. I'll go with you.

MAGGIE. No, you'd hate him. It's sweet of you to offer, but I can't enjoy a concert with someone beside me who's hating all the time.

ELEANORE. I'd try and like it.

MAGGIE. I know you would, dear, you'd try ever so hard, but I'd be feeling apologetic and with Angel one must never feel that.

HENRY. What about me?

MAGGIE. } You?

ELEANORE. } Henry!

HENRY. I know I'm not quite up to Angel but I'm much nearer than Eleanore is and I'm ready to go farther.

MAGGIE. It's terrible nice of you to offer, Henry, but—no.

ELEANORE. Such a cold night—and you have a cold.

HENRY. I haven't. And I liked that German jazz thing, Maggie, I did indeed, and the Gershwin piano concerto—I wasn't stupid about it, was I, Maggie? I believe I'd enjoy Avila.

ELEANORE. I'm certain you wouldn't.

HENRY. Don't be too sure. I've been steeping myself in seventeenth- and eighteenth-century music; I'm getting a bit tired of it, a bit tired of your cups of clear, cold water, Eleanore. I'm all for cocktails and liqueurs to-night.

MAGGIE. Bravo, Henry!

ELEANORE. Cocktails are most unwholesome at your age, Henry.

HENRY. At my age? You talk as if I were an old man.

ELEANORE. Well, you're middle-aged. Too old to alter your tastes.

HENRY. Maybe I'll find some link between the most modern and Scarlatti—another touch for the book.

MAGGIE. Stravinsky has his eighteenth-century period.

HENRY. So I've heard.

MAGGIE. And Angel often plays Stravinsky.

HENRY. Then I'll go, dashed if I don't.

MAGGIE. Hurrah! I'll let you off the dancing afterwards.

HENRY. I can't dance.

MAGGIE. I know. That's why I let you off. Hat and coat instanter.

HENRY. Oh, I'm not properly dressed.

MAGGIE. That doesn't matter. I'm dressed enough for two.

ELEANORE. Aren't you very tired, Henry, after working all day?

HENRY. I've hardly done a stroke; anyway the music will revive me. Just a minute, Maggie. (*He dashes from the room.*)

MAGGIE. I hadn't the heart to discourage him, Eleanore. The concert won't last very long and we'll come straight home.

ELEANORE. It's only that I'm worrying

about his health.   He's been out so much lately, gadding here and there with you and working so hard at that blessed book.   I hate to seem to be a damper but I know better than you do what he can do and what he can't.

MAGGIE. I'll give up the concert, I don't care about it as much as that.

ELEANORE. No, go my dear, go.   I wouldn't spoil your evening for anything, and anyway Henry's set his mind on going and once he's made up his mind he's as obstinate as a mule. Here he is, he wasn't long.

> (HENRY *comes in, he has got into an over-coat and a muffler, he has* MAGGIE'S *cloak over his arm.*)

HENRY (*quite excited*). This was in the hall. It's right, isn't it?

MAGGIE (*getting into it*). Perfectly right, Henry.

HENRY. By Jove, I'll feel quite conceited being with you to-night.   Everyone will be wondering why the young beauty picked up the shabby old man.

MAGGIE. Old man, fiddlesticks!   We'll be back by half-past ten or a very little later, Eleanore.   Let's have lots of tea then.

ELEANORE. Very well.   Lots of tea.   Good-bye.   Enjoy yourselves.

> (*They go out.*   ELEANORE *thinks hard for a minute, then she goes to the phone and dials a number.*)

ELEANORE. Is that Doctor Boeson? Mrs. Swinnerton speaking. . . . How are you? I'm sorry to disturb you but are you very busy just now? . . . Oh, good. Would it bother you awfully to come up and see me for a few minutes? . . . No, it's nothing serious, you needn't bring a black bag. . . . No, it's not myself. . . . Oh, do you think so? As a matter of fact I've not been sleeping very well lately. . . . Oh, just worried, I'll tell you why when you come up. . . . Are they quite harmless? I have a dread of drugs, sleeping things I mean, never took one in my life. But that's not the point, I want to see you about something quite different. . . . You'll be up in a few minutes? Thank you so much.

> (*She rings off and moves away but almost immediately the phone rings. She goes to it.*)

Oh yes, Arthur. . . . Clarke's changed his mind again, not coming till ten? What a man! . . . Yes, no, I mean. Maggie's not gone, she's writing in her little room. . . . No, the concert's not till nine, you've plenty of time. You can be here in ten minutes, can't you? . . . Yes, you mistook the hour. . . . Well, you'd have three quarters of an hour of Avila anyway and I'm sure that will be half an hour more than you can stand. Anyway, come and talk it over with Maggie. . . . Right. (*She rings off.*)

> (*She moves about the room nervously,*)

*powders her nose, waits for the doctor
who a minute or two later is announced
by Julia. He is a rather ordinary man,
not very intelligent outside his pro-
fession.)*

JULIA. Dr. Boeson. (*She goes.*)

ELEANORE (*shaking hands*). Kind of you to
come up so quickly, Doctor Boeson.

BOESON. Not at all, I had nothing to delay
me and I'm only one flight down.

ELEANORE. Do sit down.

BOESON. Where are the family?

ELEANORE. They've gone to a concert.

BOESON (*sitting*). Cold, isn't it?

ELEANORE. Bitter.

BOESON. Well, what's the trouble?

ELEANORE. I'm very worried about my
husband.

BOESON. What's wrong with Henry?

ELEANORE. He's overworking, he's wearing
himself to a rag.

BOESON. Oh, I can hardly believe that.

ELEANORE. I know what I'm talking about.
You don't know him well, you don't see him as
I do, day after day; this Scarlatti book—it's
killing him, he's putting his whole heart and
soul into it, it—it—— (*She can't go on.*)

BOESON. I know he's been writing hard for
the last year.

ELEANORE. Eighteen months.

BOESON. As long as that?

ELEANORE. Yes, and years of research before, verification of manuscripts, translations—oh, you've no idea what work those things entail.

BOESON. A lot, I suppose.

ELEANORE. Ordinary people like you—forgive me, Doctor Boeson—I mean people who don't know by experience seem to think that a work of biography entails much less strain than, say, a novel.    But the contrary is the case.    The strain is much greater, the strain of casting yourself back into a past century, a dead society.

BOESON. Yes, of course.    But in a way I should have thought that your husband was rather peculiarly fitted for "casting himself back" as you call it.    He seems to me, if I may say so, a little old-fashioned, not quite of our rushing century.

ELEANORE. You're right, he was like that, oh yes, he was.

BOESON. But now?

ELEANORE. This book is his life.    He has been dreaming of it for years.    I can see, if I look at it coolly, that it's all nonsense.    What does it matter whether Scarlatti's life is done again and done well or ill?    But for him it matters enormously, and for me because I love him, I can't bear to see him fail.

BOESON. Why should you think he will fail?

ELEANORE. I'm afraid for his health.    Just at the end, just when the book needs the finishing touches, I see him flag; he gets tired so easily, he has these constant colds, they make him ready to accept the second-best in himself. Oh, I suppose I seem to be talking foolishly but I have lived with him for more than twenty years and I know him through and through. I want you to help me, Doctor Boeson.

BOESON. How?

ELEANORE. He must lead a very quiet life.

BOESON. Quiet? Henry never seemed to me exactly—noisy.

ELEANORE. He must take things easy.

BOESON. But he seems a pretty strong man. Not very robust of course, but wiry.

ELEANORE. He is not a young man.

BOESON. Of course not.

ELEANORE. He looks younger than he really is. He is a middle-aged man. He thinks he can do the things that young men do. I wish you could see him—medically. I wish you could scare him a little about himself.

BOESON. I see. Frankly, Mrs. Swinnerton, I think you are frightening yourself unnecessarily about your husband. I think——

ELEANORE. I'm not, I know I'm not. Oh, you doctors lie so often to us when we're dying and tell us we're going to get well; can't you for once lie in the other direction? But it won't be a lie, alas, I know it won't. He's wearing himself out body and soul and I'm the only one who sees it.

BOESON. Your daughter doesn't agree with you?

ELEANORE. Maggie knows nothing about him; she's only been home three months. Before that she hadn't seen him for three years.

BOESON. I haven't been seeing much of him this winter myself; you seemed such a happy trio I didn't like to bother you by dropping in as I used to do. Suppose I take up the old custom and come up to-morrow night for a chat? I could look at him—unprofessionally—and see how the land lies.

ELEANORE. Oh, do, do.

BOESON. That's settled then. And now about yourself.

ELEANORE. Myself?

BOESON. You're not—quite the thing, are you?

ELEANORE. Oh, I'm all right.

BOESON. You seem strung up, nervous.

ELEANORE. Worrying about Henry.

BOESON. You said you weren't sleeping.

ELEANORE. Not very well.

BOESON. How long has this been going on?

ELEANORE. I don't know. For the last couple of months I think.

BOESON. What's the cause of it?

ELEANORE. Worry, I suppose.

BOESON. I see. (*He takes out a little bottle.*) Will you take one of these little tablets to-night and one to-morrow night and one the night after and see what happens?

ELEANORE. I told you I hated those sort of drugs. I'm very old-fashioned, I'd rather not.

BOESON. Do you drink tea?

ELEANORE. Of course. Lots.

BOESON. Well, tea is a drug—of the other kind. Instead of having tea to-night have one of those, they're very harmless.

ELEANORE (*who has spilled them into her hand*). They're certainly very small, probably that makes them the more deadly.

BOESON. They're not a bit deadly. If you swallowed twenty of them they wouldn't kill you and there are only ten here. But even one little fellow will help you to go to sleep, and I promise you'll wake with no hang-over.

ELEANORE. I'll think about it but I won't promise. I prefer my tea.

BOESON. I think—if you'll forgive my saying so—your anxiety for your husband is a bogy in your mind; you're not well yourself and that makes you think that he is ill. It's quite likely he has been overworking; I'm sure he needs a holiday and I'm certain that you do. Couldn't he drop the book for a month? Change, travel, that's what you both want. How long is it since you've been abroad?

ELEANORE. Not for three years.

BOESON. Then that's the thing for you. Preferably go to some country where you can't understand the newspapers and only know enough of the language to feed yourselves and ask the way.

ELEANORE. But I'm a hopeless traveller, I'm ill all the time.

BOESON. Oh, that's unfortunate.

(ARTHUR TALBOT *presents himself. He is thirty-six, quite pleasant if a trifle ordinary.*)

ELEANORE. Good-evening, Arthur.

ARTHUR (*breathless*). Good-evening, Mrs. Swinnerton.

ELEANORE. Is there anything the matter?

ARTHUR. Sorry. The lift-man wasn't there and I ran up.

ELEANORE. All those stairs! No wonder you're blown—you know Dr. Boeson, don't you?

ARTHUR. Yes, of course. Good-evening, doctor.

BOESON. Good-evening, Talbot. How are the roads getting along?

ARTHUR. I'm trying to forget such things exist. Where's Maggie?

ELEANORE. She'll be here in a minute.

BOESON. I thought you said she and Henry——

ELEANORE (*rising*). It was so kind of you to look in, Doctor Boeson; I'm ashamed of myself for bothering you. I'll remember what you said.

BOESON (*rising, feeling himself dismissed*). It

24

was no trouble at all.    I'll come up to-morrow evening after dinner.    And take that little pill.

ELEANORE. Maybe.    We'll look forward to seeing you anyway.

BOESON. Good - night, Mrs. Swinnerton. 'Night, Talbot.

ARTHUR. Good-night.

(*Boeson goes out.*)

ARTHUR. I say, aren't you well?

ELEANORE. Do I look ill?

ARTHUR. You look stunning.    But the pill?

ELEANORE. Indigestion, Arthur.    Do sit down.

ARTHUR (*sitting*). Thanks.    Where's Maggie? Oughtn't we to be off?

ELEANORE (*sitting too*). Maggie's gone.

ARTHUR. Gone?    But you said on the phone——

ELEANORE. I know.    (*She smiles a charming, disarming smile.*)    I told you a lie.    She had gone when you phoned, gone to the concert with her father; unfortunately you were just too late.

ARTHUR. But—but why did you say she was here?

ELEANORE. Because I wanted to have a little talk with you and I knew you were expecting that Mr. Clarke at ten and if you thought there was only me here you wouldn't think it worth while to come over.

ARTHUR. Oh, I say, Mrs. Swinnerton, if

you told me you really wanted to see me, I'd have come like a shot.

ELEANORE. I wonder, would you. Anyway, it doesn't matter; you're here and that's the main thing.

ARTHUR. I always like being here, Mrs. Swinnerton.

ELEANORE. And we like having you.

ARTHUR. You've all been so decent to me, I don't know what my leave would have been like if it hadn't been for all of you.

ELEANORE. We've all grown to be very fond of you, Arthur.

ARTHUR. Nice of you to say that.

ELEANORE. I've lots more to say to you and I find it very hard to begin.

ARTHUR. I say, I'm not a very terrifying person, am I?

ELEANORE. No.

ARTHUR. Then go ahead, it can't be anything so very dreadful.

ELEANORE. It's—it's like this. Henry is wrapped up in his work, he doesn't notice things, he doesn't care—you know how he is.

ARTHUR. Yes, but he's a grand chap.

ELEANORE. Of course. But he leaves me to do lots of things that he should do.

ARTHUR. Yes. I know you run everything here.

ELEANORE. And now I've got to run you.

ARTHUR. Me?

ELEANORE. We're quite old-fashioned people, Henry and I.   And now I've got to behave like a really old-fashioned father.   I'm—— *(She hesitates)*.

ARTHUR. Yes?

ELEANORE. I'm going to ask you what your intentions are regarding Maggie.

ARTHUR. My intentions?

ELEANORE. Maybe you have none, in that case it's all right, though maybe a little heartless towards her.

ARTHUR. I—I don't quite understand.

ELEANORE. It's not of course that you've compromised her in any way or even got her talked about, but—well, it's just that.   What *are* your intentions?   She's coming home from the South of France, she joins your boat at Marseilles, you strike up a friendship, she brings you here, we all like you, we become good friends.   But Maggie—what about her?

ARTHUR. You'd like to know whether I want to marry her?

ELEANORE. Yes.

ARTHUR. I have thought of it, yes, I have. But I said "No, she's not for me".

ELEANORE. Why should you say that?

ARTHUR. She's so young, she's so modern, she's written this brilliant, successful novel. Imagine her in a little hill-station in India! Why, we're only just beginning to discover the Forsyte Saga.

ELEANORE. She likes you very much.

ARTHUR. Does she? Oh, we're good friends, I know.

ELEANORE. *Very* much.

ARTHUR. Don't think I haven't imagined her there, coming home in the evening after tennis. Dinner—they *can* cook, those fellows, with a couple of braziers and a little charcoal; maybe after dinner I'd read to her or she'd read to me, or there'd be the gramophone or—no, no, it's absurd, Mrs. Swinnerton; if you'd ever been in a little hill-station in India you'd know how absurd.

ELEANORE. I know she's written a brilliant novel, but she's not really that awful thing a "modern girl". You see since she was twelve she's lived in the South of France, very quietly, at one school after another. It happens that her novel is about the Riviera, but it's not about fast people, it's not Cannes, it's not Nice, it's not Monte Carlo, it's just the honest South of France as she knew it.

ARTHUR. I know she's not just "a modern girl". But Gharobi—can you picture it? We have amateur theatricals three times a year: an Edgar Wallace mystery play five years old, an early Maugham, some ten-years-old farce. As to music—nothing. Braga's "Serenata" is as near as we come to the Big Bs. No one knows who the Big Bs are—or if they knew they'd be bored to tears by Bach and Brahms. I get on

28

all right because I'm pretty ordinary myself, but even I sometimes realise how narrow and behind the times we are. Imagine asking Maggie to come out and share that life! I've thought of it, Mrs. Swinnerton, indeed I have, and realised it was impossible.

ELEANORE. Bach, Beethoven, Brahms—they matter like anything when you're in love, or they don't matter at all.

ARTHUR. You mean she's really in love with me?

ELEANORE. I think so. I'm not sure.

ARTHUR. I don't dare to believe it.

ELEANORE. You're too modest, Arthur. If you weren't awfully nice, do you think we'd have had you here, day in, day out?

ARTHUR. Another thing, I haven't a very big salary; I couldn't give her all she's accustomed to.

ELEANORE. We're not rich, as you know, but I could allow Maggie four or five hundred a year. Henry has no money; anything we have is mine, and I can do what I like with it. We could take a smaller flat; it would be worth stinting ourselves a little to know that Maggie was happy.

ARTHUR. Her happiness is the main thing.

ELEANORE. She's not living a wholesome life here. We gave up that little room to her (*indicating the door at the back of the stage*). She locks herself in, and writes there at all hours of

29

the day and night. She even has a little bed there and sleeps there sometimes and gets up in the middle of the night and writes. The few young people she has got to know——well, you've seen them. I suppose I'm old-fashioned, but I don't like them; they have no morals, no stability. If she stays here, she'll probably marry one of them—for a year—for a day. Your dull hill-station sounds so safe and sane.

ARTHUR. Oh, we're awfully moral! . . . How old is she?

ELEANORE. Twenty-one her next birthday.

ARTHUR. And I'll be thirty-six.

ELEANORE. Arthur, that doesn't matter, that matters least of all. It doesn't matter with a man, with a woman, yes, oh yes.

ARTHUR. God, if it could come true. But I'm sailing in two weeks, and I daren't put off going even for one week.

ELEANORE. Henry and I got married within ten days. Oh, Arthur, I want her to be happy, I want her to be happy.

ARTHUR. If I could make her happy!

ELEANORE. You can; yes, you can.

(*The door opens and there are* MAGGIE *and* HENRY.)

ELEANORE. Why, whatever——?

MAGGIE. A motor-smash.

ARTHUR. ⎫ Maggie!
ELEANORE. ⎭ Henry, you're hurt?

30

HENRY. We're all right.

MAGGIE. Oh, we weren't in it. It was Angel, poor darling Angel on his way to the concert got bumped into by another taxi. Thank goodness his precious hands weren't injured, but he was all shaken up, so the concert had to be cancelled.

ELEANORE. How disappointing.

MAGGIE. Oh well, he'll live to play another day.

ARTHUR. Did you get your money back?

MAGGIE. Now isn't that practical of you, Arthur. Of course I didn't.

ARTHUR. Why not?

MAGGIE. Because, my dear boy, my tickets were comps. Oh, Eleanore, you should have seen old Susie Fisher trying to get back money on two comps. she had bought at half-price from a friend. But what are you doing here, Arthur? What's happened to old Clarke?

ARTHUR. Put me off again. He's coming at ten.

MAGGIE. He's incorrigible.

ARTHUR. Utterly.

ELEANORE. Are you cold, Henry? Come to the fire.

HENRY. Not a bit cold, thanks.

ELEANORE. I'm glad, after all, the concert fell through. You'd have been very tired, fit for nothing to-morrow.

HENRY. Maybe. But I'd like to have

heard Avila all the same. I think I'll go and do a little work.

ELEANORE. At this hour?

HENRY. It's not really late, and I did practically nothing to-day; Maggie had the manuscript.

ARTHUR. I thought it was finished, or almost finished.

HENRY. Maggie thinks there are things that can still be done to it.

ELEANORE. What sort of things?

HENRY. Oh, brighten it up a bit, you know. Local colour and all that sort of thing.

ELEANORE. How can you get local colour when you don't know the localities. You've never even spent a week-end in Naples.

HENRY. That's just it. I think I've got to know them. Maggie and I were talking about it again in the cab coming home.

ELEANORE. Talking about what?

HENRY. Going out there—to Sicily and Naples—and getting local colour.

ELEANORE. Are you crazy? That kind of knocking about would kill you. You know what a bad traveller you are.

HENRY. I know what a bad traveller *you* are, my dear. That's the only thing that makes me hesitate. Do you think you could ever stand it.

ELEANORE. How ill you were crossing from Boulogne the last time.

HENRY. Yes, but what a crossing, the worst

in years they said, and I was all right an hour after we landed, but you didn't get over it for a week.

ELEANORE. I remember.   How can people joke about such things?

HENRY. The worst of it is I believe only small steamers call at Trapani, and the blue Mediterranean can be uncommonly grey and rough on occasion.

MAGGIE. The steamers aren't so very small, Henry.

ELEANORE. No, no, it's an impossible idea, and you shouldn't encourage him in it, Maggie.

MAGGIE. I only said I thought the book wanted a little brightening up.

HENRY. You said I should go and see those places.

MAGGIE. Did I?   Yes, I believe I did.

ELEANORE. The book is perfect as it stands, perfect.   Sober, well documented, full of new material.   I believe people are getting tired of these modern bright biographies.

ARTHUR (*looking at his watch*). I think I ought to be going.   It would be just like Clarke to get it into his head to come a bit earlier.

MAGGIE. Oh, must you, Arthur?

ARTHUR. 'Fraid so.   Anyhow the dancing is out of the question, worse luck.   Clarke is certain to jaw for a couple of hours.   I'm awfully sorry, Maggie, I have let you down to-night.

MAGGIE. It wasn't your fault.   I'll go and

33

do a spot of work.    Remember we've a date to-morrow evening, dinner and a theatre.

ARTHUR. Right oh! I won't fail.    Good-night, Mrs. Swinnerton.

ELEANORE. Good-night, Arthur.

ARTHUR. I'll—I'll think over what you were telling me.    Good-night, Maggie.

MAGGIE. Till to-morrow and, mind, no excuses about Mr. Clarke.

ARTHUR. He has to go to-morrow, thanks be.    'Night, Henry.

HENRY. I'll see you out.    What about a spot before you go?

ARTHUR. No thanks.

*(The men go out.)*

MAGGIE. I'm awfully sorry, Eleanore, if I've upset Henry's mind about the book, but he asked me my honest opinion.

ELEANORE. I wouldn't mind if he was strong enough for that sort of thing but he isn't.

MAGGIE. He's not really ill, is he?

ELEANORE. I don't know, I hope not. I know he's far from well.    In fact, I had a talk with Doctor Boeson to-night, and he's coming up to-morrow evening to have a sort of informal look at him.

MAGGIE. Really?

ELEANORE. He's not as young as he once was, and he won't realise it.

MAGGIE. He always seems so young, almost my contemporary.

34

ELEANORE. And this cold he has—you don't notice it in the daytime, but at night he just coughs and coughs.

MAGGIE. Does he?   How dreadful.

(HENRY *comes back*.)

HENRY. And now the little writers must get to their books.   What did you do with the manuscript, Maggie?

MAGGIE. It's in your study.

HENRY. Thanks.   (*To* ELEANORE) Well, old girl, are you prepared to face the Mediterranean with me?

ELEANORE. No, Henry.   Don't be silly.

HENRY. Then I'll take Maggie with me.

ELEANORE. You'll take—Maggie?

HENRY. Yes.   She tells me she never was ill at sea in her life.   She'll hold my hand and administer brandy at the crucial moment.

MAGGIE. I won't go with you, Henry.

HENRY. Why not?   You said earlier in the evening that if Eleanore refused you'd come.

MAGGIE. I've changed my mind. I don't believe you ought to go.

HENRY. Why not?

MAGGIE. You're not well.

HENRY. Not well?   This is some notion of Eleanore's.

ELEANORE. It's Eleanore's, but it's not a notion.

HENRY (*suddenly getting obstinate*). I'm perfectly well and I am going.

ELEANORE. You're not.

HENRY. You can't stop me.    Eleanore, you and I are a pair of old fogies, we're behind the times.    Maggie has given me a new view of things.    She's right about the book, every minute I see more and more how right she is. If neither of you will come with me, I'll go alone.

ELEANORE. That would be quite crazy.

HENRY. I know a certain amount of Italian, I'd get on all right.

ELEANORE. It comes to this: you'd like a holiday away from me.

HENRY. No, no, you mustn't think of that, old girl.    But I'd hate to think you were being made ill all the time by those beastly trains and steamers and the queer cooking.

ELEANORE. You'd hate to drag round an old, sick wife.

HENRY (aghast). Eleanore!    How can you say such a thing?

MAGGIE. I think I'll go and do a little work. I'll probably sleep down here, Eleanore. Good-night all.

(She goes rather quickly through the door
at the back.)

HENRY. You shouldn't say such things, and before Maggie.

ELEANORE. What does Maggie matter? They're true.

HENRY. They're not.

36

ELEANORE. But the other thing is true too, that you couldn't stand the journey.

HENRY. That remains to be proved. I'm going.

ELEANORE. Where will you get the money?

HENRY (*after some seconds of amazed silence*). Do you mean to say you wouldn't give me——? Never, Eleanore, in all the years we have been together have you reminded me that—oh, how can you do it now?

ELEANORE. I'll stoop to anything hateful to stop you. I'm horribly worried about you, Henry. That journey would kill you.

HENRY. Nonsense.

ELEANORE. You're overtaxing your strength. You're no longer a young man, remember that.

HENRY. I'm forty-four, that's not old. Everyone tells me I look thirty-five.

ELEANORE. You're so vain you're taken in by any stupid remark like that.

HENRY. I feel under forty—most of all since Maggie came home. When we go out together it's almost as if we were the same age.

ELEANORE. Pah!

HENRY. Of course I'm not, I know that. Eleanore, you seemed to be making me older than my years. Maggie makes me feel younger. Well, it's nicer to feel younger.

ELEANORE. It's disgusting to see old men behaving like overgrown schoolboys.

HENRY. Meaning me?

37

ELEANORE (*getting half-hysterical*). You'll be having electric baths soon and injections to keep you sprightly. Everyone will be laughing at you behind your back and you'll be too conceited to notice them.

HENRY. Eleanore, what's come to you to-night, you're talking quite crazily?

ELEANORE. You're the crazy one. Poor old gadabout Henry!

HENRY (*after a pause*). I'm going to the study. No use our talking when you're in this sort of mood.

(*He goes towards the door.*)

ELEANORE (*following him and throwing her arms round his neck*). Oh, forgive me, Henry, forgive me. It's only that I love you so much. Can't you see that? Forgive me and give up this wild-cat idea.

HENRY. Of course I forgive you. (*But he breaks from her arms.*)

ELEANORE. And you won't go?

HENRY. I'm almost certain I will. You're not the only one in the house that has money.

ELEANORE. I—I'm not the——?

HENRY. Maggie has a nice fat cheque due to her from her publishers.

ELEANORE. You'd take Maggie's money?

HENRY. Why not? She'd be the first to offer it—especially if we go away together.

ELEANORE. You—with Maggie?

HENRY. Yes, with Maggie.

(*He goes out.*)

(ELEANORE *sits down and thinks for a minute in utter misery. Then muttering, "It can't be, it mustn't be", she goes determinately to* MAGGIE'S *door. She tries the handle, but the door is locked. She knocks sharply on it.*)

MAGGIE'S VOICE. Who's there? Who is it?

ELEANORE. Eleanore. I want to come in. I must see you.

MAGGIE'S VOICE. Oh, all right. I'll unlock the door.

(*A little pause and the door is unlocked.* MAGGIE *is in a dressing-gown and slippers.*)

MAGGIE (*holding the door open*). Is anything the matter?

ELEANORE. I have something important to say to you.

(*She passes into* MAGGIE'S *room, the door closes behind her and the curtain falls.*)

# ACT II

SCENE: MAGGIE'S *room.   The room is smaller than
the room in Act I. and much shallower—it is
really an inner drawing-room.   On the left
is a fireplace filled up now by a gas-stove;
there are chairs on either side of the fireplace.
At the centre back is a door leading into the
room of the first Act.   On the right is a
window and along the wall stretching from
the upper right corner is a low bed, hardly
looking like a bed, more like a couch; it is
covered with some gay stuff; the end of the
bed probably protrudes under the window.
There are a few small book-cases filled with
books and a few pictures, mostly gay water-
colours of the French Riviera or Italy.   In
the centre of the room is a largish workman-
like table with a typewriter on it and many
papers.   There is a chair at the table with
its back to the audience.   Between the head
of the bed and the door is a rack on the wall
with some hooks, and as the curtain rises*
MAGGIE *is hanging up the dress she has been
wearing in Act I.   A dark dress hangs on
another hook.   She herself is in a pretty*

*dressing-gown. The dress hung, she takes off her shoes and gets into a pair of bedroom slippers. She crosses to the table, lights a cigarette and sits down with her back to the audience. She puts a piece of paper into the typewriter and is beginning to copy from a page on the table when there comes a sharp rap on the door.)*

MAGGIE. Who's there?  Who is it?

ELEANORE'S VOICE. Eleanore, I want to come in.  I must see you.

MAGGIE. Oh, all right.  I'll unlock the door.  (*She goes to the door and unlocks it.*)

MAGGIE (*holding the door open*).  Is anything the matter?

ELEANORE (*outside*).  I have something important to say to you.

(*She comes into the room.*  MAGGIE *closes the door.*)

ELEANORE. I'm sorry to disturb you, darling, but I can't help it.

MAGGIE. Have a cigarette.

(ELEANORE *takes one.*  MAGGIE *lights a match.*  ELEANORE *can hardly light her cigarette, her hands are trembling.*)

MAGGIE. Why, your hands are shaking. Are you cold?

ELEANORE.  This room is like an ice-house.

MAGGIE. I'll light the gas.  (*She does so.*`

ELEANORE. Is the window open?

41

MAGGIE. Just a scrap.

ELEANORE. Shut it, please.

MAGGIE (*shutting it*). Right oh! but I warn you the little room will be all fug in five minutes.

ELEANORE. We can open it again.

MAGGIE. Do sit down. You look very— very tired.

> (ELEANORE *sits above the fireplace.*
> MAGGIE *on the chair centre hitching*
> *it round so that she can see* ELEANORE.)

ELEANORE (*after a pause*). I've several things to say to you. First, I want to apologise for that little scene a minute ago. I shouldn't have spoken as I did. I lost control of myself for a moment.

MAGGIE. That's all right.

ELEANORE. The fact is — I'm not very well.

MAGGIE. I thought you were looking a bit seedy to-night.

ELEANORE. I've not been sleeping. When I got Doctor Boeson up to talk to him about your father he was much more interested in my health. He insisted on giving me these. (*She shows the bottle of tablets.*)

MAGGIE. What are they?

ELEANORE. Things to make me sleep. He says they're quite harmless, but I have a dread of those sort of things.

MAGGIE. Oh, do take them; it's awful not to sleep.

ELEANORE. Maybe I will — but I didn't come to talk about my health, only I thought I'd tell you that as a sort of excuse for my stupid behaviour.

MAGGIE. If you could get a few good night's sleep I bet you'd be as right as rain.

ELEANORE. Perhaps so. What matter? . . . Weren't you surprised to see Arthur to-night?

MAGGIE. Yes, a little. It hardly seemed worth while his coming round as he had to be back so soon to meet Mr. Clarke. Had he been here long when we got back?

ELEANORE. He telephoned just after you had gone and when I told him you had left he said he'd come round anyway as he wanted to see me. I was very surprised.

MAGGIE. Arthur's very fond of you, he admires you tremendously—why shouldn't he. You're very attractive, Eleanore.

ELEANORE. Oh, he didn't come for my beauty and charm. *You* were the sole topic of conversation.

MAGGIE. I was?

ELEANORE. Yes, my dear. Are you surprised?

MAGGIE. A bit. What had you both to say about me?

ELEANORE. Can't you guess?

MAGGIE. No.

ELEANORE. He's very much in love with you.

MAGGIE. Oh!

ELEANORE (*after a pause*). Is that all you have to say?

MAGGIE. It's rather surprising. I never thought of such a thing. We're very good friends of course.

ELEANORE. It seems to me a very natural culmination of the friendship.

MAGGIE. Does it?

ELEANORE. I confess I suspected it, only I wasn't sure he'd have the courage—I'm not even sure yet that he will. Arthur's not exactly shy, but he's got no self-confidence and he's very much afraid of you.

MAGGIE. Why on earth should he be?

ELEANORE. He thinks you're very brilliant—and of course you are. He thinks he's very commonplace and dull and that he could only offer you a very commonplace and dull life.

MAGGIE. Do you mean he seriously wants to marry me?

ELEANORE. Yes.

MAGGIE. What did you say?

ELEANORE. I said I knew you liked him very much, beyond that I couldn't go. As a matter of fact Arthur's not commonplace and dull, he's really rather a profound person, with a great deal of delicate feeling. He surprised me to-night.

MAGGIE. I think it's all just a bit of sentimentality on Arthur's part. Coming home after being abroad for so long, and we were

44

practically the only friends he made. He'll forget me before he's a week on the ship.

ELEANORE. I don't think so.

MAGGIE. He'll fall in love with some nice girl on the boat, and if he's still in the marrying mood they'll get married in Bombay.

ELEANORE. You won't consider the idea at all?

MAGGIE. 'Fraid not.

ELEANORE. I'm sorry. Your father and I are so fond of him. Poor Arthur!

MAGGIE. I'm sorry too. But as I say, he'll get over it.

ELEANORE. Not very quickly, I think. It's a little stupid of you, Maggie, to call him a sentimentalist; that's just the last thing he is. He's very sensitive and he's very practical, that's why he hesitates to ask you.

MAGGIE. What's there practical in not asking me?

ELEANORE. He thinks you'd find life in India dull and behind the times—the European part of it, I mean.

MAGGIE. I'm sure I should. His description of it was pretty ghastly.

ELEANORE. And then he was afraid he hadn't enough money to make you really comfortable. I said we could let you have five hundred a year.

MAGGIE. Eleanore! That's fearfully generous of you. You could never afford that.

ELEANORE. Oh yes we could, if it was to make you happy.

45

MAGGIE. I couldn't take it from you.

ELEANORE. Why not?

MAGGIE. I don't know, I just couldn't. . . . Does Henry know about this?

ELEANORE. I haven't had a chance yet of talking it over with him, and there's no need to, it's simply a matter between you and Arthur; but I promised to put in a good word for him.

MAGGIE. I must say I feel rather bowled over.

ELEANORE. Are you in love with anyone else?

MAGGIE. Gracious, no. I've never been in love in my life.

ELEANORE. I think you should consider Arthur. He won't be all his life in that dull little station. I've always wanted so much to see India.

MAGGIE. Yes, but for keeps! No, my life is here, in this little room, writing, and Henry—and you.

ELEANORE. You'd soon get sick of it and us—two old people.

MAGGIE. I don't think so, I'm very happy here. I've a quiet disposition really, I don't want a lot of entertainment. I'm really, though I may not look it, an Old-fashioned Girl.

ELEANORE. That's what I told Arthur.

MAGGIE. You encouraged him?

ELEANORE. I certainly didn't discourage him. Why should I? I told him there was no harm in his trying. What else could I say? Especially when your father and I like him so much.

46

MAGGIE. But, Eleanore, he's years older than I am.

ELEANORE. Not so very many. He thought of that. I told him it doesn't matter if the man is older. If it's the other way—maybe.

MAGGIE. You have an answer to everything.

ELEANORE. I try to look at things coolly.

MAGGIE. I don't feel you so cool about this; there's a quiet drive behind everything you say.

ELEANORE. I'm thinking of your future.

MAGGIE. You seem awfully anxious to get rid of me and you haven't had me with you so long—only three months.

ELEANORE. Darling, what things you say.

MAGGIE. What things *you* say.

ELEANORE. I assure you I'm only thinking of your happiness. (*She gets up.*) I'll say no more, Maggie, all I ask is that you'll think this thing over very seriously. Don't give Arthur a hasty refusal. I want you to be happy. When I came in here I meant to say all kinds of eloquent things to you but I seem tongue-tied, but—I want you to be happy. Good-night.

(*She is at the door.* MAGGIE *rises.*)

MAGGIE. Stop.

ELEANORE. What is it?

MAGGIE. Don't go yet.

ELEANORE. I've said my say.

MAGGIE. I've not said mine. (*Slowly*) It's only just forming in my mind.

ELEANORE. But I don't want you to come to

any decision about Arthur until you've had time to——

MAGGIE. It's got nothing to do with Arthur.

ELEANORE. What on earth are you thinking of?

MAGGIE. You want me to be happy, Eleanore. Do you, I wonder?

ELEANORE. Of course.

MAGGIE. Sit down again, Eleanore, let's get this thing clear.

ELEANORE. I don't know what you're——

MAGGIE. Sit down.

(ELEANORE *sits in the same chair*, MAGGIE *doesn't sit.*)

MAGGIE. Eleanore, when did you begin to want my happiness so badly?

ELEANORE. Always, Maggie.

MAGGIE. I wonder. For the last three years I've been begging and begging to be allowed to come home and you always refused.

ELEANORE. I had to think of your education, darling, and look at the result—your brilliant novel. Wasn't I justified?

MAGGIE. You knew nothing of it until it was finished.

ELEANORE. I always had great hopes of you.

MAGGIE. Kept out there year after year like something one was ashamed of, like a love-child —a by-blow.

ELEANORE. Maggie!

MAGGIE. That's what the other girls began

48

to think I was, somebody's bastard, kept at school after I was grown up, and then the year at that horrible *pension*.   It was a queer way of making me happy, Eleanore.

ELEANORE.  I did it for the best; I think you're rather ungrateful.

MAGGIE.  I'm trying not to be, I'm trying to puzzle something out.   I worshipped you when I was a child, Eleanore, you were so beautiful—you are still of course.

ELEANORE.  Pooh, I'm an old woman.

MAGGIE.  I worshipped you, and you loved me.

ELEANORE.  Naturally.   You were a charming child.

MAGGIE.  Then you turned on me—suddenly.

ELEANORE.  Nonsense.

MAGGIE.  Yes, you did.   When was it?  Yes, when I was eleven or twelve, and you sent me away, you suddenly didn't want me near you. Why?   What had I done?   I suppose I was a horrid leggy little girl, but no more horrid than most little girls.

ELEANORE.  You're being quite ridiculous, Maggie.   There came a time when you had to go to school like all little girls.

MAGGIE.  Henry liked me; we were getting to be great friends, we used to go long walks together in the country, he was teaching me botany—do you remember, Eleanore?

49

ELEANORE. Of course.

MAGGIE. And then there was that summer—
I wanted to go to the sea and you hate the sea
and——

ELEANORE. And we went to the sea.

MAGGIE. Yes. And we used to go boating
and fishing and you could never come because
you'd get ill.

ELEANORE. Yes.

MAGGIE. And next term I was packed off to
France and I only saw you and Henry twice in
eight years—not even let come home for the
holidays—and I'd be there still if you had your
way, but you can't keep a girl of twenty permanently banished like a child, not if she can
make money by little stories and articles as I did
and buy her own ticket home.

ELEANORE. "Permanently banished"—what
nonsense you're talking.

MAGGIE. You promised to take me home
three years ago, that time you and Henry came
to see me. Why didn't you, Eleanore, why
didn't you?

ELEANORE. I——

MAGGIE. No, don't answer me. I'm trying
to piece this all together myself. Let me remember; you were ill the day after you came, the
result of the train journey. Then you got all
right, the three of us were together for two days,
then you got ill again—or said you were ill—
and shut yourself up in your room for the rest

of the time and Henry and I went everywhere
together, got fun out of the same kind of things,
went to the casino, stayed up late; he bought me
two pretty little frocks. Yes, Eleanore, I see, I
see it all now; it's Henry.

ELEANORE. What do you mean—Henry?

MAGGIE. He's behind it all, behind all your
cruelty to me—for you *were* cruel, Eleanore.
You're jealous of Henry loving me so much,
that's it, you can't deny it.

ELEANORE. I can, and do.

MAGGIE. And now that I've come home he
loves me more than ever and I love him and we
both get fun out of things you don't like at all,
but I'm too old to be sent back to school so now
you grab at this chance of marrying me off,
sending me thousands of miles away so that
Henry will only see me once in five years.
That's your scheme now, isn't it, Eleanore?

ELEANORE. I'm thinking of nothing but your
happiness.

MAGGIE. Oh, for God's sake stop talking
about my happiness. Let's have this thing out
fair and square. Be honest, Eleanore. You
hate me, you know you do. Can't you say so,
straight, and be done with it?

ELEANORE (*getting up*). You don't know what
you're saying. I'm going.

MAGGIE (*catching her and holding her*). Tell
me the truth. Out with it, Eleanore.

ELEANORE. No.

MAGGIE. I'm Jacob with the angel; I'll not let you go until you curse me.

ELEANORE. You really want it? Very well, I'll say it. I hate you. I wish you were dead.

MAGGIE (*as if she had been struck*). Oh!

ELEANORE. You've taken Henry from me. You're making a fool of him, dragging him around, flattering him, making him think himself twenty-one. I could laugh till my sides ached at the two of you—if I didn't want to cry.

MAGGIE. Eleanore!

ELEANORE. Can't you call me "mother"? Why don't you? You used to. I'm sick of you and your "Eleanores" and "Henrys". He's your father, I'm your mother; will you please not forget that.

MAGGIE. I'll go away.

ELEANORE. Yes, go, go.

MAGGIE. You'll never see me again.

ELEANORE. I hope not.

(*There is a knock at the door.*)

ELEANORE. Ssh! Was that a knock?

(*The knock is repeated.*)

MAGGIE. Come in.

(HENRY *appears.*)

HENRY. Is anything the matter? You were talking so loudly I could hear you in my study.

ELEANORE. Nothing is the matter. What should be?

HENRY. Sure?

ELEANORE. You'd better go back to the study or, better still, go to bed, it's very late.

HENRY. Oh, it's not so late. Are you coming?

ELEANORE. In a few minutes. Don't wait for me.

HENRY. Anything up, Maggie?

MAGGIE (*with a contemptuous inflexion on the first word*). Mother and I have been talking things over, Henry. I've decided to leave.

HENRY. Leave? Leave here?

MAGGIE. Yes.

HENRY. In the name of goodness, why?

MAGGIE. Oh—because.

HENRY. But I thought we were all so happy together.

MAGGIE (*with a tremor*). So did I.

ELEANORE. We forget that Maggie's no longer a child, Henry; she can come and go as she pleases.

HENRY. Yes, of course. And she wants to go?

ELEANORE. Yes, Don't you, Maggie?

MAGGIE. Will you please go away, both of you. (*She sits down dejectedly.*)

HENRY. I'm hanged if I go till I've cleared this thing up. Why is Maggie going, Eleanore?

ELEANORE. Because she wants to. We're too old.

*53*

HENRY. Maggie, why do you want to leave us?

(MAGGIE, *her face in her hands, just shakes her head.*)

HENRY (*going to her and kneeling beside her*). Maggie, darling, what's wrong? Are you bored here? I don't believe you are. It's something else. I'll do anything to make you happy. Don't cry, darling, don't. Look here, we'll go away for a month, just you and I, to Sicily and those other funny places, and when we come back everything will be all right again. Oh, don't cry, Maggie, don't cry, and don't mind Eleanore, she's not herself to-night. I love you, Maggie, you know I do. Don't you, don't you?

MAGGIE (*flinging her arms round his neck in a burst of weeping*). Oh, Henry, Henry!

HENRY. Hush, hush. We'll go out first thing in the morning to one of those travel places and find out all about steamers and trains—I'll have to get a thin suit but I'll buy me a reach-me-down so as not to delay our going—why we might be able to go to-morrow night, my passport's all right. Eleanore thinks I oughtn't to go but she'll really be glad to get rid of me for a bit, it'll give her a rest. I believe I've been getting on her nerves with my silly old book; she must be sick of it. Stop crying, Maggie, stop crying.

ELEANORE (*getting HENRY away and taking his*

*place with her arms round* MAGGIE). Will you please go away, Henry.

HENRY.  Go away?

ELEANORE.  Yes, you've utterly upset Maggie.

HENRY.  I was trying to quiet her.

ELEANORE.  You've not succeeded very well.

HENRY.  But what's the matter?   What have you been saying to her?

ELEANORE.  Please go away.

HENRY.  But——

ELEANORE.  Do as I ask you.   We can talk about your travels in the morning.   Please go away now.

HENRY.  Well, if you insist——

ELEANORE.  I do.

HENRY.  Very well.   Good-night, Maggie.
          (*And, rather reluctantly, he goes.*)

ELEANORE (*sharply*).  Maggie, stop crying, pull yourself together.

MAGGIE.  I'm—I'm sorry.
          (*With an effort she controls herself, gets up, crosses the room and sits on her bed.*)

ELEANORE.  Probably you won't believe me, but I'm very sorry for you.

MAGGIE (*dully*).  That's all right.

ELEANORE.  I said I hated you.   I don't think that's true, but Henry comes first.

MAGGIE.  That's natural of course.

ELEANORE.  Perhaps we'll never have another opportunity of talking out straight to each other.

There are things I want to say to you. You said a little while ago "Let's get this thing clear", and then you told the story in your own way, from your own point of view. Now I want you to hear my side of it.

MAGGIE (*after a pause, dully*). Well, what is your side?

ELEANORE. I'm an old woman.

MAGGIE (*startled*). Eleanore, what are you talking about?

ELEANORE. I'm an old woman. I'll be sixty-two next month.

MAGGIE. No one would ever believe it.

ELEANORE. And I feel sixty-two—no, I feel older.

MAGGIE. That's because you're not well.

ELEANORE. Henry was twenty-three when we were married, I was forty, that's twenty-one —nearly twenty-two—years ago. He was mildly in love with me, I was frantically in love with him—I am still. Oh, Maggie, whoever you marry, never marry a man younger than yourself. It's hell. It was all right for the first eight or ten years, then I felt myself wanting to slip into a comfortable middle-age—but Henry had only just turned thirty. You must remember him as he was when you were a little girl, his gaiety, his boundless energy.

MAGGIE. Yes, indeed, I remember.

ELEANORE. And how horribly attractive he was to other women.

56

MAGGIE. When I was a child I thought him fascinating.

ELEANORE. Of course. There was one year —you were eight or nine I think—I wasn't very well and I let myself go slack. Henry went to places alone. He started an affair with a woman a few years younger than himself. If I hadn't pulled myself together I'd have lost him. I was horribly frightened. I saw that to keep him I'd have to work hard. I set myself deliberately to do two things, to make myself appear younger than I was and to make him seem older. Thank goodness I have never let my figure go; I was still slim; I had the remains of whatever beauty I ever had—oh, it wasn't so difficult to seem twelve or fifteen years younger than I really was, I had a certain charm, fascination, call it what you will. I could keep men hanging about me, keep Henry up to the mark, make him jealous sometimes—but it wasn't so easy to make Henry think himself old.

MAGGIE. That time at the sea he seemed to me quite an old man, but of course I was looking at him through a child's eyes.

ELEANORE. He wasn't old then, he isn't now, of course, but you're right, by that time—that was four years later—he was tamed. He had had a bad attack of pneumonia and I got him to believe that as a result one of his lungs was a little affected. I pretended to be very anxious about his health and he was very fond of me; he was ready to do anything to please me—or rather *not* to do a lot of things to please me and at last I felt safe again.  I was able to relax and take things a bit easier—and then you began to grow up.

MAGGIE. I was only a little girl.

ELEANORE. But a very precocious, intelligent one.  I was very proud of you, I loved you very much, I loved you for your pretty ways and your active little brain—until Henry began to make you his companion.  You loved all the things that he loved and I hated, the sea and long country walks and grubbing for wild flowers. You were in the house every day—do you remember we had a governess for you but he taught you half the time?—you were under his eyes, ready to be his companion at any minute, and he began to slip away from me again.  I persuaded him to let me send you to a boarding-school; it was no use, he counted the days to the holidays, looking forward to them more than you did I expect, and those holidays were a torture.  I was shut out of Henry's life almost completely, I was shut out of yours. More and more you became his child.

MAGGIE. Poor mother.

ELEANORE. So I sent you to France.  Does this all sound high-flown and ridiculous?  Looking back on it now it does, but what could I do? Lose Henry?

MAGGIE. Didn't you exaggerate the importance of our companionship? What was I? A horrid little schoolgirl of twelve.

ELEANORE. Unfortunately you weren't a bit horrid, and every year would have made you more his companion. Those two visits we paid to you in France proved that; you fitted into each other like hand into glove, I was left utterly in the cold.

MAGGIE. Otherwise—apart from me—was it all right?

ELEANORE. Yes, utter peace, utter safety. I encouraged him to write, first those two small books of criticism, then this Scarlatti book, they kept him busy, tied him down—till now.

MAGGIE (*bitterly*). Till I came home.

ELEANORE. Till you came home and the whole thing started over again worse than ever.

MAGGIE. It's an ugly story.

ELEANORE. It's a very miserable one.

MAGGIE. I'm glad you've told it to me, Eleanore, it's made things much clearer. And now let me tell you something . I believe you're crazy, crazy on this particular point. I mean I can quite understand your getting anxious long ago about those other women—or that woman—but Henry and I! That seems complete hay-wire. What does it matter if we occasionally go out together to some concert you wouldn't enjoy or to watch some tennis championship? That's only a couple of hours out of the twenty-four, you have him all the rest of the time.

ELEANORE. Oh, it's not that particularly, but —he's only forty-four, you see, he said to-night he felt under forty and that you had made him feel like that.

MAGGIE. You mean you don't feel safe?

ELEANORE. No.

MAGGIE. Is there another woman?

ELEANORE. No. But there may be. And I can't begin the old game of pretend again, I can't. I'm too old, I'm too tired. We had settled down so happily into being a middle-aged couple.

MAGGIE. Goodness, I'd let him gallivant and philander if he wants to. No man is worth bothering that much about.

ELEANORE. Henry is.

MAGGIE. I'm sure he's not. I don't like you, Eleanore, but you're worth ten of him.

ELEANORE. Nonsense.

MAGGIE. He's awfully fond of you. I believe you're scaring yourself unnecessarily.

ELEANORE. I wish I could believe you. You've made me so miserable and frightened. And I had felt so safe.

MAGGIE. Well, let's get down to brass tacks. I'm going, of course.

ELEANORE. I can't pretend I want you to stay.

MAGGIE. But we must move warily. Henry must never know why I go.

ELEANORE. I'd be lost for ever if he knew.

MAGGIE. But I go only on one condition.

ELEANORE. What is it?

MAGGIE. That Henry and I make this trip abroad together.

ELEANORE. Never. I won't ever allow that.

MAGGIE. You must.

ELEANORE. No. Why should I?

MAGGIE. For two reasons. The first is that it will throw dust in Henry's eyes if you seem very happily to consent to our going away together. That will save your face. Afterwards I shall say that I've decided to live in the South of France.

ELEANORE. And what's the other reason for your going away with Henry?

MAGGIE. Because I adore him. My God, Eleanore, do you think you're the only one who loves him? He was my idol when I was a child. I loved him as a girl, all those years in France—only two visits in eight years, remember—I never forgot him. Now you're asking me to give him up for life and I've consented. I've said, "Yes, I will". But I can't leave him like this—just to-morrow. I can't, Eleanore, I can't. I want some splendid memory of him, something that will last me all my life.

ELEANORE. Very well. We'll go away, the three of us.

61

MAGGIE. No. I won't have that. I must have him all to myself for a month.

ELEANORE. Never.

MAGGIE. Oh yes, you've got to agree to my terms. I can be as hard as you, Eleanore, and I hold the whip hand. I have only got to tell Henry why I am going.

ELEANORE. You'd never do that?

MAGGIE. Yes I will, like a shot, if you try to stop me. I've plenty of money, thanks to my foolish novel. We're quite independent of you, Eleanore. (*She suddenly laughs, half hysterically.*) If Henry could only hear us wrangling over him! Isn't it like "The Playboy"? "Two fine women fighting for the likes of me." Who'd think to look at Henry that he was so fascinating? However, Eleanore, those are my terms.

ELEANORE. I don't accept them.

MAGGIE. Very well, I leave to-morrow and I tell Henry why.

ELEANORE. No, please, Maggie, please.

MAGGIE. Those are my terms and I don't go back on them.

ELEANORE (*violently*). Very well, I accept them. But you'll be sorry. I'll make you pay in some way; I don't know how, but you'll pay.

MAGGIE. Oh, don't be so melodramatic.

ELEANORE. I'm not. You'll laugh the other side of your mouth before long, see if you don't, and maybe sooner than you expect.

MAGGIE (*getting off the bed and going for a cigarette*). You know, Eleanore, you are crazy. There's been some queer kink in you always. (*She sways a little on her feet.*) Oh, my head's swimming. I'm not strong enough for these big emotional scenes; you're better at them than I am, Eleanore.

ELEANORE. Poor darling, it's all my fault. I told you I wasn't quite myself to-night. Please, don't do any work to-night, slip into bed.

MAGGIE. Do you imagine I could write a line after a scene like this?

ELEANORE (*sitting beside her on the bed*). You're in pyjamas, aren't you? (*She opens her dressing-gown.*) Yes. Come, into bed with you. (*She slips off the dressing-gown and tucks her into bed.*)

MAGGIE (*in a collapsed voice*). I feel utterly exhausted, but I wonder if I'll sleep.

ELEANORE. I'm sure you will. Happy thought! What about one of these sleeping tablets? Have you any scruples about such things?

MAGGIE. None. I often take a Dial Ciba.

ELEANORE. Doctor Boeson said these were quite harmless. Is there any water in the room?

MAGGIE (*sleepily*). There's a carafe and a glass on the top of the little bookcase.

ELEANORE. I have it. (*She pours some water into the glass and brings it to the bed.*) Here.

63

MAGGIE (*holding out her hand for the tablet*). Goodness, that's three you're giving me.

ELEANORE. I want to be sure you'll sleep. Doctor Boeson said if I took twenty of them they would do me no harm.

MAGGIE. Oh, very well. (*She takes them and a drink of water.*)    Thanks.

> (ELEANORE *puts back the glass and moves about the room tidying it, hanging up the dressing-gown, etc.*)

MAGGIE (*sleepily*). Where's Henry?    I want Henry.

ELEANORE. He's gone to bed.

MAGGIE. I wish he'd come, I want to talk to him. . . . What are you doing?

ELEANORE. Only tidying the room.

MAGGIE (*after a pause*). Is the window open?

ELEANORE. Yes.    You opened it; don't you remember?

MAGGIE. Did I?

ELEANORE. Yes.

MAGGIE (*after a pause*). Oh, Eleanore, I forgot.

ELEANORE. What?

MAGGIE. The door, it's not locked.    I can't sleep in a room that's not locked.    I was attacked once in France——

ELEANORE. Don't stir; don't worry.    I'll lock it after me when I go out.    I'll leave the key with Julia.    You can ring the bell for her in the morning when you want to get out.    Will that do?

MAGGIE. Perfectly.

> (*There is a long pause.* ELEANORE *turns out the gas. It makes a pop.*)

MAGGIE (*almost asleep*). What was that?

ELEANORE. Turning out the gas.

MAGGIE. Oh.

> (*Another pause.* ELEANORE *turns on the gas but doesn't light it. It makes a faint hissing. She gets up, goes to the door, opens it, turns off the light in* MAGGIE'S *room. Her figure is silhouetted against the light of the sitting-room. She is going out, she hesitates, comes back, switches on the light again, looks at* MAGGIE, *looks at the gas-fire, her face contracts in hatred, she switches off the light, goes out rapidly and the key can be heard turning in the lock.*)

# ACT III

*The same scene as Act I. The time is the morning after Act II.* HENRY *is very happy at the fireplace with guide-books, time-tables, and maps.* JULIA *is dusting the room. The door on the left stands open.*

HENRY (*after a moment*). Are you sure you'll hear the bell?

JULIA. Miss Maggie's? Yes, sir. I've left the door open on purpose to hear it.

HENRY. She's not often as late as this, is she?

JULIA. It's not eleven yet. She often sleeps late if she's been writing till all hours the night before.

HENRY. I wish she'd wake up. . . . (*He goes back to his guide-books.*) Julia, do you know what an omnibus train is?

JULIA. I'm sure I don't, sir. Maybe it's a train that meets a bus somewhere.

HENRY. Oh, perhaps so. . . . And *couch-ettes*, what are they? . . . I say, there's a train that leaves Boulogne at 12.20—oh, it doesn't seem to go beyond Amiens, how stupid of it.

But if one gets to Calais at 14.25—good Lord, what hour is fourteen. I hate these times that go round and round the clock, and then there's daylight saving to think of—I give it up, Maggie must figure it out.

JULIA. Are you going away, sir?

HENRY. Yes, Miss Maggie and I are going on a little trip, to Sicily and those sort of places.

JULIA. And is the mistress staying on here?

HENRY. I expect so. Where is she now by the way?

JULIA. I think she's in the study, sir. (*A bell rings.*)

HENRY. Ah, that must be Miss Maggie at last.

JULIA. No, sir. It's the front door, sir.

> (*She goes out.* HENRY *busies himself with his guide-books. A minute later* ARTHUR *comes in.*)

ARTHUR (*in great spirits*). I had to blow round. I've just put him into his final taxi. I was so glad to see the last of him I almost kissed him.

HENRY. Morning, Arthur. Who the devil are you talking about?

ARTHUR. Clarke, of course. He's gone, he's really gone. Where's everyone?

HENRY. Eleanore's around somewhere, in the study I think. Maggie hasn't put in an appearance yet.

ARTHUR. I say, she's a lazybones, isn't she?

67

HENRY. Well, not really. She works very late sometimes and then is late in the morning, but she's never as late as this.

ARTHUR. I hoped she'd come out for a spin in the car with me and have lunch somewhere in the country. Do you think she'd come?

HENRY. Probably—unless she wants to do a morning's work, but that's not likely if she worked late last night.

ARTHUR. I feel like a kid out of school— Clarke being gone. I feel I've a whole holiday. I wish Maggie would come.

HENRY (*ringing a bell*). I'll talk to Eleanore about it; I'm sure we can persuade her to go. You know, Arthur, I'm feeling like you this morning—kiddish and holidayish. Maggie and I are planning a trip together.

ARTHUR. Oh! . . . The trip you were talking of last night?

HENRY. Yes, to Sicily and all the Scarlatti places. Eleanore won't come, so Maggie and I are going together.

ARTHUR. I see.

HENRY. I'm trying to look up trains and things, but I can't make head or tail of them. Are you any good with continental time-tables?

ARTHUR. Not much, I'm afraid. Did Eleanore say nothing to you last night about —about me?

HENRY. I can't remember; I don't think so. What should she have said?

ARTHUR. Well, about me and Maggie.

HENRY. You—and Maggie?

ARTHUR. Yes. I want awfully to marry her.

HENRY. Arthur!

ARTHUR. Are you surprised?

HENRY. Somehow I never thought of Maggie marrying.

ARTHUR. I know I'm not half good enough for her, but Mrs. Swinnerton seemed to think I had a chance. Are you—what do you think?

HENRY. Maggie marrying? Going away? To India?

ARTHUR. Does it seem so dreadful?

(JULIA *appears*.)

JULIA. You rang, sir?

HENRY. Oh yes. Will you ask your mistress to come here if she's not very busy.

JULIA. Yes, sir.

(*She goes out.*)

HENRY. Arthur, you've rather knocked me out. I never thought of such a thing.

ARTHUR. I had, but I put it out of my mind; I thought it wasn't possible. Mrs. Swinnerton makes me think it is. I was very stupid about it last night, scared and—and just stupid. But this morning I feel quite cocky and confident— the result of old man Clarke being off my shoulders, I expect. Do you think—what do you think Maggie will say?

HENRY. You wouldn't want to marry her at once, would you?

ARTHUR. Well, I have to leave in ten days at latest.

HENRY. Ten days? You'd take her back with you?

ARTHUR. Yes, if she'll come.

HENRY. Oh. . . . Then our trip would be off?

ARTHUR. 'Fraid so. We'll do it—the three of us—on my next leave.

HENRY. I see. . . . Her coming home had made such a difference; you can't imagine what a difference it had made to me. I was getting awfully humdrum and old, she woke me up. But if she is to get married I'd rather it would be to you than anyone else I know.

ARTHUR. Thank you, Henry.

(ELEANORE *comes in. She looks very tired and old.*)

ELEANORE. You wanted me?

HENRY. Here's Arthur. He wants Maggie to go out in the car with him.

ARTHUR. Good-morning, Mrs. Swinnerton. I was wondering whether Maggie wouldn't come out for a drive with me and have lunch.

ELEANORE (*vaguely*). Maggie?

HENRY. I was telling him we haven't seen her yet to-day.

ELEANORE. No, we haven't seen her yet.

HENRY. You know, Eleanore, I think we ought to knock her up.

ELEANORE (*quickly*). No, no, please don't do that.

70

HENRY. She doesn't generally sleep so late.

ELEANORE. Oh, let's wait, let's wait.

HENRY. But she's going to miss a nice drive. Has she ever slept as late as this before?

ELEANORE. I told you—Doctor Boeson's sleeping-stuff.

HENRY. I forgot. But even still——

ARTHUR. What's that? What about sleeping-stuff?

HENRY. Well, she wasn't feeling very well last night, thought she wouldn't sleep and so Eleanore gave her a couple of sleeping pills.

ARTHUR. She seemed all right when I left her.

HENRY. Yes, it was afterwards. Wasn't it, Eleanore?

ELEANORE. Yes. Afterwards.

ARTHUR. I hate people taking that sort of dope.

HENRY. Boeson swore they were very harmless. Didn't he, Eleanore?

ELEANORE. Yes.

ARTHUR. How many did you give her?

ELEANORE. Three.

ARTHUR. Three! That's quite a dose.

ELEANORE. I took two myself.

ARTHUR. Did you sleep?

ELEANORE. No. Not for one instant.

HENRY. These things affect people differently. Maggie'll probably sleep the clock round. You'll have to give up your drive, Arthur.

ARTHUR (*indicates the room at the back*). Is she sleeping in there?

HENRY. Yes.

ARTHUR. Couldn't you peep in, Mrs. Swinnerton, and see if she's still asleep?

HENRY. The door is locked.

ARTHUR. Locked?

ELEANORE. She always locks her door.

HENRY. But on this occasion the key's outside. You locked the door, didn't you, Eleanore? And gave the key to Julia. She has only to ring the bell and Julia will go to her.

ARTHUR. But suppose she's ill, too ill to ring?

ELEANORE. You're being quite absurd, Arthur. Why did you come this morning?

ARTHUR. I told you. To take her for a drive.

ELEANORE. Oh yes, it's very kind of you.

ARTHUR. I wish you'd unlock the door and take a look in.

HENRY. Yes, why shouldn't we, Eleanore?

ELEANORE. No, no, please don't. She— she may be writing, she gets so annoyed if she's disturbed. Or maybe she didn't go to sleep till late. Oh, let her sleep. Isn't sleep the most wonderful thing in the world?

ARTHUR. You look as if you wanted a good night's sleep, Mrs. Swinnerton. You're not looking a bit the thing this morning.

ELEANORE. I'm perfectly all right. I remember now, I slept quite a lot last night. Why shouldn't I?

ARTHUR. I'd like everyone to be in the best of form to-day. I've told Henry, Mrs. Swinnerton, about—about Maggie and me, what—what I hope for.

ELEANORE. Yes?

ARTHUR. He was a bit surprised, but on the whole he doesn't disapprove. Do you, Henry?

HENRY. Certainly not. I'll miss Maggie terribly. We both will, won't we, Eleanore?

ELEANORE. Of course.

HENRY. We'll have to settle down into two old people.

ARTHUR. Maybe she won't say "yes". . . . Somehow it seems to me to be horrible for us to be talking about Maggie and she to be locked in that little room unable to get out. If you'd just unlock the door, you needn't go in unless you want to——

ELEANORE. No, Arthur, please——

HENRY. Why not, Eleanore?

ELEANORE. Oh, as you will.

HENRY. I rather agree with Arthur; it would be pleasanter to feel she was able to come out whenever she wanted to. I'll call Julia, she has the key.

(*He opens the door and calls* JULIA.)

ARTHUR. Thanks. You must think me awfully fussy. But I'm unlike Maggie, I have a kind of horror of being locked into a room.

73

HENRY. Maggie got a bad scare in France once and ever since she locks her door.

ARTHUR. If we're going to have a good spin before lunch, we ought to be starting quite soon.

HENRY. If she's asleep, we're not going to wake her, are we, Eleanore?

ELEANORE. No.

(JULIA *appears.*)

HENRY. Oh, Julia, the key of Miss Maggie's room, please; Mrs. Swinnerton wants it.

JULIA. Here it is, ma'am.

(*She hands it to* ELEANORE *and goes out.*)

HENRY. Now, Eleanore, release the prisoner and set Arthur's mind at rest.

ELEANORE (*tries to rise but can't*). You—you take it, Henry.

HENRY. Why?

ELEANORE. I'd rather.

HENRY. Oh, very well. (*He takes the key.*)

ARTHUR. You look quite ill, Mrs. Swinnerton. Can I get you anything—a glass of water?

ELEANORE. I'm all right.

(*She sits with her back to* MAGGIE'S *door, her hands to her head, almost shutting her ears.* ARTHUR *watches* HENRY, *who goes to the door and gently turns the key in the lock.*)

ARTHUR. Look in and see if she's awake.

ELEANORE (*in a choked voice*). No . . . no . . . Henry.

HENRY. What did you say, Eleanore?

ELEANORE. Nothing.

> (*Very cautiously* HENRY *opens the door a crack, then wider.*)

HENRY. Why, Maggie, we were wondering what had become of you. Do you know what hour it is?

MAGGIE (*coming slowly into the room.*) I'm very late, I know.

> (*She is dressed in the dark dress we saw hanging on the hook in her room. She is very pale. Her right wrist has a handkerchief tied round it. The handkerchief is stained with blood.* ELEA-NORE, *with a little stifled cry, rises and backs away from her.*)

ARTHUR. Maggie, you look like a ghost.

MAGGIE. Like something back from the dead?

HENRY. You're not ill, are you?

MAGGIE. No.

HENRY. What about some breakfast?

MAGGIE. I'd like a cup of tea.

HENRY (*ringing the bell*). I'll get Julia.

ARTHUR. What happened your wrist?

MAGGIE. I cut it.

ARTHUR. How?

MAGGIE. I broke a pane of glass; it's nothing.

ARTHUR. I want you to come out in the car and have lunch with me. Will you, Maggie?

MAGGIE. That sounds nice, Arthur.

HENRY. Do you think she looks well enough to go, Eleanore?

ELEANORE. I—don't know.

MAGGIE. Why shouldn't I be well enough— Mother?

(*Without replying* ELEANORE *sits down again.*)

ARTHUR. A blow of fresh air is what you want.

MAGGIE. Yes, fresh air sounds lovely.

(JULIA *appears.*)

HENRY. Make some tea for Miss Maggie, please, Julia.

JULIA. Very well, sir.

(*She goes out.*)

(ELEANORE, *suddenly, with a swift movement gets up and leaves the room.*)

ARTHUR (*startled*). I don't think Mrs. Swinnerton is well. She looks ghastly.

HENRY. Do you think so? Maybe I'd better see.

(*He goes out.*)

ARTHUR. What's up this morning? You and your mother—you seem so strange. Did those beastly sleeping things not agree with you?

MAGGIE (*coming to him and laying her hand on his arm*). Arthur, she—she says you love me. Do you?

ARTHUR. Why yes, Maggie.

MAGGIE. You want to marry me?

76

ARTHUR. Yes.

MAGGIE. Could you marry me at once, take me away this minute?

ARTHUR. This minute?     What do you mean?

MAGGIE. What I say.

ARTHUR. You want to marry me?

MAGGIE. Yes.

ARTHUR. Why?

MAGGIE. The usual reasons, I suppose.

ARTHUR. I don't believe you love me a bit.

MAGGIE. I'm very fond of you.

ARTHUR. Only that?

MAGGIE. Arthur, take me away.

ARTHUR. What's the matter.     You're frightened?

MAGGIE. Terrified.

ARTHUR. Why?   What's happened?

MAGGIE. I'll never tell you. Listen, I'm very fond of you but I don't exactly love you. Maybe it's better that I shouldn't; love seems such a terrible thing. But I'll do my best. Only trust me, take care of me, take me away this morning, now—at once.

ARTHUR. This morning?

MAGGIE. For God's sake don't fail me, Arthur. I know it all seems mad and disorderly—and you're so orderly. Thank God you are. You're the only sane solid thing I know of in the world. Don't fail me now.

ARTHUR. I won't, Maggie, you can depend

on me.   You took me aback for a minute.   I
don't suppose we can get married to-day, but we
can get married very quickly.

MAGGIE.   I could go away, couldn't I, to
some hotel and wait until you had everything
fixed up?   I must get away from this place, I
can't spend another night here.

ARTHUR.   What will Henry and Eleanore
say?

MAGGIE.   I don't care; it doesn't matter what
they say.   Have you got your car here?

ARTHUR.   Yes.

MAGGIE.   Good.   (*She rings the bell.*)

ARTHUR.   There's a quiet little hotel just
round the corner from my place.

MAGGIE.   I'll go there.   And, mind, not a
word to anyone till I'm safely out of this.

ARTHUR.   All right.

MAGGIE.   You're a dear, Arthur.   This must
all seem cock-eyed to you.   Any ordinary person would pester me with a hundred questions.

ARTHUR.   I thought I was awfully ordinary.

MAGGIE.   I don't believe you are.   Maybe
it's not so ordinary nowadays to be sane and
steady.   I think we'll get on terribly well together.

(JULIA *comes in.*)

MAGGIE.   Don't mind about the tea, Julia.   I
forgot, I'm going away for the week-end and
I've only just time to catch my train.   Will you
pack the small suit-case as quickly as you can?

78

Just the usual things, that blue dress will be all I want.

JULIA. Very well, Miss. Shall I ring for a taxi?

MAGGIE. No, Mr. Talbot will take me to the station. But hurry, Julia, I must be out of this in five minutes.

JULIA (*hurrying out*). Yes, Miss.

MAGGIE. Doesn't it seem mad?

ARTHUR. On the contrary, awfully sensible.

MAGGIE. How long have we till you sail?

ARTHUR. Ten days if I go overland to Marseilles—only a week if I go by long sea.

MAGGIE. Let's go by long sea.

ARTHUR. Right. It won't give you much time to get things.

MAGGIE. I don't need things. Can you marry a wife who has just one suit-case and a big bundle of manuscripts?

ARTHUR. Rather.

MAGGIE. I can get things in India, Arthur, can't I? All the same, I'm sure I'll disgrace you.

ARTHUR. By Jove, I must do some cabling to get things a bit ready for you.

MAGGIE. Let's dump my bag at the hotel and then go miles and miles and miles into the country.

ARTHUR. Fine.

MAGGIE. Marrying doesn't matter; I mean we can see about that to-morrow. I've lots of

money, enough to buy a special license or whatever it's called.

(ELEANORE *comes in, she is excited.*)

ELEANORE. What's Julia doing, Maggie?
She's rushing about your room flinging things
into a suit-case. What is it? Are you going
away? If Henry gets to know——

MAGGIE. Eleanore, Arthur is here.

ELEANORE. I know. I've seen him already.
But Maggie, if you go away like this Henry
will suspect, he'll think——

MAGGIE. I am going away this morning.
And I'm going to marry Arthur.

ELEANORE. Oh!

ARTHUR. Won't you wish us luck, Mrs.
Swinnerton?

ELEANORE (*mechanically*). Of course. I hope
you'll both be very happy.

ARTHUR. I'll do my best to make Maggie
happy.

ELEANORE. I wished for this, you know I
did, Arthur. But—but why must you go like
this, in this sudden way? Maggie——

MAGGIE. Be quiet, Eleanore. Arthur, will
you go and talk to Henry for a few minutes?
Don't tell him anything.

ARTHUR. Right oh!

MAGGIE. Call me when Julia has my bag
ready.

(ARTHUR *goes out.*)

MAGGIE. Eleanore, I hoped to have got

80

away without seeing you, unfortunately that's not possible. The less I say the better. Just understand this; it would be physically impossible for me to stay another night in this house after—after last night. You can tell Henry whatever lie you like to explain why I've gone.

ELEANORE. You won't tell him?

MAGGIE. No.

ELEANORE. Thank you. You're generous, Maggie. . . . I think I was out of my mind.

MAGGIE. I hope you were.

ELEANORE. What happened?

MAGGIE. To make you do as you did? I don't know.

ELEANORE. I didn't mean that. What happened after—after I left you?

MAGGIE. Well, I didn't die, anyway.

ELEANORE. I know. But I wonder why not.

MAGGIE. I never went quite to sleep, I just dozed; the sleeping stuff I suppose started to work, and then—the gas. I smelt it for a long time before I realised what it was—I was so doped; when I did realise what it meant I knew in a flash that you—you——

ELEANORE. That I had turned it on?

MAGGIE. Yes. Somehow I knew from the first that you had lied to me about the window, when you told me it was open I knew at the back of my mind that it was still shut. I had the sense to know that the first thing to do was

81

to get some air. I tried to open the window, I was too dazed and dizzy, so I smashed the pane with my hand.

ELEANORE. And cut your wrist?

MAGGIE. Yes. Then I crawled across the floor on my hands and knees and managed to cut off the gas.

ELEANORE. You might have bled to death. How horrible!

MAGGIE. Why should you think it horrible? You wished me dead.

ELEANORE. Somehow it would have been horrible—that way.

MAGGIE. Instead of bleeding to death—it was a slight cut—I fell asleep on the floor.

ELEANORE. And slept till just now?

MAGGIE. No, I woke at six.

ELEANORE. Why didn't you ring for Julia?

MAGGIE. I had a great deal to think over, Eleanore, and I had the cruel feeling that I wanted to make you a little uncomfortable. Why should I let you know at once that your plan had failed? *Were* you uncomfortable, Eleanore?

ELEANORE. In hell.

MAGGIE. I'm glad.

ELEANORE. What am I to do now? All's lost?

MAGGIE. On the contrary you have everything. What more do you want? All the cards are in your hand. I'm going across the world; I shall never see you again, I hope.

You've only got to make up some convenient lies to satisfy Henry. You're a good liar, Eleanore, and Henry's very easily fooled.

ELEANORE. Somehow I'm tired of that, I don't feel I can do it any more. I'd like to tell Henry the truth.

MAGGIE. Is he big enough to stand it?

ELEANORE. Of course he is.

MAGGIE. He's charming—but, I wonder.

(ARTHUR *comes in*.)

ARTHUR. Julia is almost ready, she says. I can't find Henry. Let's go down to the car, Maggie.

MAGGIE. Very well. I've a hat in here, I think.

(*She goes into her room.*)

ELEANORE. Arthur, be very good to her. I haven't been—always. I think some day she'll forgive me.

ARTHUR. I'll be good to her, but I don't know what you're talking about. I think you've been wonderful always, one of the most wonderful women I've ever known.

ELEANORE. Oh! Wonderful!

ARTHUR. Anyway, you've helped to make me the luckiest man in the world.

ELEANORE. I don't think you'll ever change your mind.

ARTHUR. You bet I won't. If only Maggie will agree with me!

(MAGGIE *comes out, putting on her coat.*)

83

MAGGIE. I'm ready. I'll let you know, Eleanore, where I am staying, so that you can send on my things.

ELEANORE. Very well. I'm going to tell him, Maggie.

MAGGIE. Please yourself. But you're taking a risk.

ELEANORE. Ah no, you don't know Henry.

MAGGIE. As you please. Come Arthur.

(*They go out.*)

(*There is a moment's pause, then the phone rings.* ELEANORE *goes to it.*)

ELEANORE. Yes, it's Mrs. Swinnerton. . . . Oh, is that you, Doctor Boeson? . . . Of course, if you like. There's only Henry and myself here just now, Maggie is going out. . . . In five or ten minutes? Yes, that will be all right.

(*Another little pause,* HENRY *comes in.*)

HENRY. I didn't know that Maggie was week-ending, Eleanore. I met her in the hall, but she was in such a hurry to get away she hadn't time to answer my questions. Where is she off to?

ELEANORE. I don't know.

HENRY. You don't know? She was going in the car with Arthur.

ELEANORE. Was she?

HENRY. You don't seem interested.

ELEANORE. I remember, she said she was going with Arthur.

HENRY. Where to?

ELEANORE. I forget.   I don't know.

HENRY. Well, that seems queer.

ELEANORE. Yes, it's queer, it's awfully queer. Sit down, Henry, I have something to tell you.

HENRY. You seem so—so serious.

ELEANORE. Sit down, Henry.

HENRY (*sitting*). Well, what is it?

ELEANORE. Maggie is going away.

HENRY. I know.   She told me so.

ELEANORE. I mean she's never coming back. Not—ever—coming back.

HENRY. Never coming—you're joking?

ELEANORE. And she's going to marry Arthur.

HENRY. Oh.   Well he wanted that.   I'm glad—though I'll miss her a lot.   But when are they going to be married?   They've not run away together, have they?

ELEANORE. In a sense — yes.   They'll be married  to-day — to-morrow — what  does  it matter?

HENRY. Eleanore,  what  the  devil's  the matter?   What has happened?

ELEANORE. I have something rather terrible to tell you and I want you to—well I want you to interrupt me as little as possible because it's very hard for me to say what I have to say.

HENRY. Yes?

ELEANORE. At first I meant not to tell you; I could have covered it up with lies—you're easily  fooled  as  Maggie  says—and  Maggie would never have told you, but I'm too tired to lie any more; it's simpler to tell you the truth. (*She pauses.*)

HENRY. Well, Eleanore?

ELEANORE. I have driven Maggie away. She is marrying Arthur to escape me.

HENRY. Escape you? What do you mean?

ELEANORE. Escape me because she is terrified of me—and with reason. I hate her. (HENRY *with an effort says nothing*.) Why don't you speak? Why don't you cry out at me?

HENRY. I'm too bewildered. You don't really mean what you say?

ELEANORE. Yes, I hate her. You have loved me, Henry, but never as I have loved you. I wanted you all to myself, all your love, all your friendship, all your companionship. I couldn't share you with anyone, not even with your own daughter.

HENRY. You mean you were jealous of our —our——

ELEANORE. Of your love for each other. Fiercely jealous.

HENRY. How ridiculous.

ELEANORE. Not a bit ridiculous.

HENRY. There was no need—it's an utterly crazy idea.

ELEANORE. You called me crazy last night, so did Maggie. Very well, I've been crazy for years—in that direction. Somehow now I feel that's all past. I feel empty.

86

HENRY. How could you have ever thought that any love I had for Maggie would alter my feeling for you?

ELEANORE. It has altered it.

HENRY. Nonsense. I——

ELEANORE. Wait. There's more to come. I tried to kill Maggie last night. (*He stares at her, unable to believe her.*) You must realise I'm telling you the truth. People do sometimes kill other people. I tried to kill Maggie.

HENRY (*after a pause, in a whisper*). How?

ELEANORE. It doesn't matter how. I didn't succeed.

HENRY (*starting up*). Eleanore! Do you know what you're saying?

ELEANORE. Perfectly.

HENRY. It isn't true, it can't be true, you're making it all up.

ELEANORE. It's quite true. I thought when you went into that room this morning you'd find her dead.

HENRY. Dead? You hoped you'd find her dead?

ELEANORE. No. I had got sane by then, but I thought it was too late.

HENRY. Dead? Maggie dead? Eleanore, awful as it sounds, I believe you're speaking the truth.

ELEANORE. I am.

HENRY. No, no, you couldn't wish Maggie dead; it's not possible.

87

ELEANORE. It's quite possible. And then I wished myself dead. If I could have killed myself this morning I'd have done so, but I couldn't think of any way except the window—and I hadn't the courage.

HENRY. Horrible.

ELEANORE. So that's it, that's the grim tale. (*She gets up, moves about the room. There is a silence.*) Have you nothing to say? (*He shakes his head.*) I wonder will you ever understand. Yes, of course you will.

HENRY. I can't take it in. That you—that *you*, Eleanore——

ELEANORE. You must take it in.

HENRY. You're something different, monstrous.

ELEANORE. Just what I always was. (*She tries to lay her hand on his arm, he shrinks away.*) Ah, you can't bear me to touch you?

HENRY. No.

ELEANORE. Nonsense. You can't do without me.

HENRY. I never want to see you again.

ELEANORE. Never?

HENRY. You've killed Maggie.

ELEANORE. I haven't. She's alive, she's going to marry Arthur.

HENRY. She's as dead as if you had shot her before my eyes.

ELEANORE. You're jealous of Arthur.

HENRY. She's dead, Maggie's dead.

88

ELEANORE. Always    Maggie,    Maggie,
Maggie.   What about me?

HENRY. You?   I don't know.   Nothing can
ever be the same again.

ELEANORE. You'll never forgive me?

HENRY. Never.   To kill Maggie!

ELEANORE. All's over, then?

HENRY. It must be.

ELEANORE. "All's over, then; does truth
sound bitter, as one at first believes?"   What's
that old poem?   You used to be fond of it.
You used to read it to me—long ago.

HENRY. It's imposible, I can't take it in.

ELEANORE. Why not?

HENRY. I can't.

ELEANORE. You could if you were a bigger
man.

HENRY. Bigger?

ELEANORE. Yes.   What a fool I've been.
I've damned my soul and my life for a little
man.   Maggie knew you better than I did.
She said, "Is he big enough to stand it?"   I
swore you were, but you're not.   You're a
little man.   You've cheated me.   All our life
together you've cheated me.   I'm ten times the
man you are.   You've charm, a sort of weak,
helpless charm, that's all you have.

HENRY. Eleanore———

ELEANORE. My God, if you'd come to me
with my story I'd have shrunk from you with
horror for a minute—as you shrunk—and the

89

next minute I'd have thrown my arms round your neck and kissed you, proud that you loved me so much.

HENRY. Horrible!

ELEANORE. All you can do is mutter words like "horrible" and say I'm mad, I'm crazy and you "can't take it in". Of course you can't because you're small, you can't contain—you can't imagine a love that's a consuming fire.

HENRY. I am taking in gradually that you are a very wicked woman.

ELEANORE. I am what I always was.

HENRY. Then I never really knew you before.

ELEANORE. No, you never knew me, Henry, but I know you now; you're petty, you're contemptible. That's my punishment.

(DOCTOR BOESON *comes in.*)

BOESON. Good-morning, Mrs. Swinnerton. Good-morning, Henry. I warned Mrs. Swinnerton that I had ten minutes to spare and would come up and smoke a cigarette—which doesn't mean that I'm not coming up again this evening. Did Mrs. Swinnerton tell you, Henry?

ELEANORE. We're so glad to see you, Doctor Boeson. Will you excuse me for a minute? I'll leave you with Henry.

(*Perfectly composed, she goes into* MAGGIE's *room.*)

BOESON. Well, how are you, Henry? It's an age since——

*fused sound from the room and* BOESON
*dashes out.*)

BOESON. Ring for an ambulance. Dial
nought.

(*He goes out very quickly.* HENRY, *with
an effort, gets to the telephone, he dials.*)

HENRY. Three storeys down. . . . Eleanore.
. . . Hallo! Ambulance. I want ambulance.
. . . Is that ambulance? There has been———
(*He speaks so weakly that evidently ambulance
asks him to speak louder. He goes on more
firmly.*) There has been—there has been—an
accident———

(*He can't continue. He drops the receiver,
it falls with a clatter and he turns away
hiding his face in his hands.*)

THE END

*May–June* 1932

# CHURCH STREET

A PLAY IN ONE ACT

Human Will and Human Fate:
What is little, what is great?
Howsoe'er the answer be,
Let me sing of what I know.

WILLIAM ALLINGHAM

The first production of *Church Street* took place on May 21, 1934, in the Abbey Theatre, Dublin, with the following cast:

| | | |
|---|---|---|
| JOSEPH RIORDAN | . . . . | Barry Fitzgerald |
| KATE RIORDAN | . . . . | Maureen Delany |
| HUGH | . . . . . | Arthur Shields |
| JACK | . . . . . | Joseph O'Neill |
| MOLLIE | . . . . . | Jennifer Davidson |
| AUNT MOLL | . . . . | Eileen Crowe |
| MRS. DE LACY | . . . . | Christine Hayden |
| MISS PETTIGREW | . . . . | May Craig |
| SALLIE LONG | . . . . . | Shelah Richards |
| JIM DALY | . . . . . | F. J. McCormick |
| HONOR BEWLEY | . . . . | Ann Clery |
| THE EVOKED HUGH | . . . | Denis O'Dea |
| DOCTOR SMITH | . . . . | Michael J. Dolan |
| NURSE SMITH | . . . . . | Frolie Mulhern |
| A CLERGYMAN | . . . . . | P. J. Carolan |

The play was produced by the Author.

# CHARACTERS

JOSEPH RIORDAN, *Manager of the National Bank, Knock.*

KATE RIORDAN, *his Wife.*

HUGH, *their eldest Son.*

JACK, *their other Son.*

MOLLIE, *Jack's Wife.*

AUNT MOLL, *Joseph Riordan's Aunt.*

MRS. DE LACY.

MISS PETTIGREW, *her Sister.*

SALLIE LONG.

JIM DALY.

HONOR BEWLEY.

DOCTOR SMITH.

NURSE SMITH.

A Clergyman.

The play begins and ends in Mrs. Riordan's drawing-room, but, on occasion, passes to Miss Pettigrew's house or Honor Bewley's bedroom, or to a doctor's waiting-room near Paddington, or to Jim Daly's lodging-house in Dublin, or to a graveyard. The period of the play varies from one evening to a few months.

# CHURCH STREET

*The scene is the drawing-room in the National
Bank, Knock. Comfortably furnished, not
overcrowded, an upright piano, a largish
table in the middle of the room. Dark wall-
paper. A fireplace on the audience's right,
a door in the middle of the wall left (leading
to the dining-room), another door in the back
wall towards the right. When the play begins
MRS. RIORDAN is poking the fire, which is
already blazing brightly; she is a pleasant-
looking, middle-aged woman. At the table
in the centre facing the audience but hidden
from them by a "Manchester Guardian"
which she is reading sits AUNT MOLL. It is
evening, and the room is brightly lit by electric
light. If a window has to be shown, it is
heavily curtained. The door at the right
opens and HUGH comes in. He is about
twenty-eight years old, dressed carelessly,
grey flannel bags, a pullover, an old tweed
jacket. His mother is quite grandly dressed
as if for an evening party. HUGH has a
tired, discontented look.*

MRS. RIORDAN. Oh, Hugh darling, there you are. Did you have a nice rest?

HUGH. No. Never slept a wink.

MRS. RIORDAN. Now, isn't that too bad? But you can get to bed early.

HUGH. What a hope! With all these awful people coming?

MRS. RIORDAN. They won't stay late. You've forgotten what early hours we keep in Knock— not like your London. They'll all be gone by ten o'clock—half-past ten at latest.

HUGH. I wish to goodness you hadn't asked them at all.

MRS. RIORDAN. Darling, they're all dying to see you, and it was the only evening I could have them this week.

HUGH (*with a little sneer*). Has Knock suddenly become so gay?

MRS. RIORDAN. Well, I don't know how it is but there seems to be something almost every night—there's badminton in the Town Hall every Wednesday, and there's the bridge club and of course the pictures; they change them twice a week, so that's two nights gone and——

HUGH. And a little party at the Moore's or the Daly's, *I* know.

MRS. RIORDAN. Anyway I had to seize this evening, you're such a fly-away; why last time you were here—four years ago—you only stayed three days, do you remember?

HUGH. I remember.

MRS. RIORDAN. Having them to-night does mean your father giving up his game of bridge at the Munster and Leinster Bank; he was a little touchy about it, but I said he must be here.

HUGH. He needn't have given it up.

MRS. RIORDAN. Maybe not. For this time you'll stay weeks and weeks, won't you? But I never can trust you. Some theatre will be wanting to put on one of your plays and off you'll fly.

HUGH. Put on one of my plays? That *is* likely, after their last experience with me.

MRS. RIORDAN. I wouldn't mind that for a minute. You can't be a success all the time.

HUGH. *All* the time!

MRS. RIORDAN. I know, darling, you haven't been properly appreciated yet, but you will be. All great writers have had to struggle just as you have. (*He contemptuously shrugs his shoulders.*) Have you unpacked your bags?

HUGH. No.

MRS. RIORDAN. You've very little time to change. They'll be here any minute.

HUGH. I'm not changing. If they don't like me as I am, they can just lump me.

MRS. RIORDAN. Oh. . . . Of course they'll like you no matter how you're dressed; but Honor's coming, and Jack's wife; she's so nice and rather smart, and I'd like the first time she sees you—I'd have your things unpacked in a jiffy. I'm sure you've a very smart London suit upstairs.

HUGH. No, don't bother.

MRS. RIORDAN (*starting to go*). No bother at all. I should have unpacked you the minute you arrived.

HUGH (*stopping her*). Please don't, Mother. It's not worth while.

MRS. RIORDAN. Not worth while?

HUGH. No. The fact is I'm—I'm not staying.

MRS. RIORDAN. Not staying?

HUGH. Well, just till to-morrow morning.

MRS. RIORDAN (*sitting down, almost crying*). But why? You've only just come. Is it a new play?

HUGH. No.

MRS. RIORDAN. Then what is it? Oh Hugh, I've been looking forward to your coming for so long.

HUGH. I know. Darling, I've a better idea. You'll come back to London with me.

MRS. RIORDAN. But—but——

HUGH. Don't you remember, two years ago, the swell time we had?

MRS. RIORDAN. I couldn't go now. Jack's going to have a baby—I mean his wife is, I must be here. What's happened? What have we done?

HUGH. Nothing. At least *you*'ve done nothing. But the place!

MRS. RIORDAN. The place? The town?

HUGH. Yes, Knock. Kay, en, o, cee, kay. My God, as I walked up from the station I could feel it closing in on me with every letter of its dull name. Its drabness, its lifelessness, dullness, dead.

MRS. RIORDAN. Of course, I suppose, after London——

HUGH. I said to myself in London, after the crashing failure of my play, "Oh, to get home again, to have some peace, to collect one's thoughts, to find a new subject, to find inspiration!" What a fool I was. I had forgotten my Knock. I realised in my five minutes' walk from the station that this place is as dead as a door-nail.

MRS. RIORDAN. You're just tired, Hugh, you're imagining things——

HUGH. I am not. I couldn't imagine anything in connection with Knock.

> (*The newspaper is suddenly slapped down, and we see* AUNT MOLL. *She is a little old woman, over seventy, plainly but not eccentrically dressed.*)

AUNT MOLL. That's the truest word you've spoken yet, Hugh me boy. You've no imagination.

HUGH (*good-temperedly*). I forgot you were there, Aunt Moll.

AUNT MOLL. Oh, everyone forgets Aunt Moll, but I'm here most of the time.

MRS. RIORDAN. Well, indeed, we don't forget you.   What a thing to say.

AUNT MOLL. With all the grand goings on to-night there'll be little thought for Aunt Moll. All I asked for was me usual glass of milk and me two Marie biscuits, but could I get them? Oh, dear me, no.   Jellies and trifles galore, but no glass of plain milk for poor old Aunt Moll.

MRS. RIORDAN. I'll see you get them.

AUNT MOLL. You needn't trouble then.   I made Maggie leave them on the sideboard for me.   If you want a thing done, do it yourself.

HUGH. Or rather, get Maggie to do it for you.

AUNT MOLL. Humph!

MRS. RIORDAN (*laughing*). As if you didn't rule the house.

AUNT MOLL. Humph!

HUGH. And so I've no imagination? That's a funny accusation to bring against a writer of stories and plays.

AUNT MOLL. You have not.   Not an ounce of it.   Walking up from the station and finding Church Street dead, moyah!

HUGH. Yes, dead.   Dead as mutton.

MRS. RIORDAN. It's early-closing day—no, it isn't.

AUNT MOLL. And would you say the same thing of Station Street and Main Street?

HUGH. Deader.

AUNT MOLL. You're a fool.

MRS. RIORDAN. Aunt Moll!

HUGH. Oh, let her fire away, Mother.

AUNT MOLL. I'm sorry, Kate, but a fool is what he is. I tell you, me boy, there's comedy and tragedy trailing their skirts through the mud of Church Street if you'd only the eyes to see them. But, oh no, not at all! You must needs write about high London society, night-clubs, cock-tail parties, things you know as much about as—as me boot. And what good does it do you? I don't suppose you've earned a hundred pounds in the seven years you've been in London.

HUGH. I got money down for my last play.

AUNT MOLL. And it ran a week.

HUGH. Anyway, it's not altogether a ques-tion of what one earns——

AUNT MOLL. Faith, I think it is. The proof of the pudding is the currants in it.

MRS. RIORDAN. It is not, Aunt Moll. Neither Joseph nor I grudge the little bit of money it costs to keep Hugh in London. We all know he's a steady boy, doesn't gamble or drink. What we spend on him is money invested and well invested. Even if he doesn't make a for-tune for himself there's the books he writes and the plays——

AUNT MOLL. Not many people seem to want to see them—or read them.

MRS. RIORDAN. That's a very unkind thing to say.

HUGH. I don't mind what you say, Aunt Moll, but mother does.  So give it a rest.

AUNT MOLL. I don't want to be unkind, Kate; you know I'm fond of the child, I know he has talent.  That's why it drives me near crazy to hear him saying a stupid thing like that.  Church Street dead!  Ha, ha!

HUGH. I wish you'd show me where it's alive.

AUNT MOLL. And I could too.  I could tell you——

(*A noise of voices and laughter outside.*)

MRS. RIORDAN. Goodness gracious, can this be them? (*She looks at her watch.*)  It is, it's half-seven.

(*The door at the back opens and admits* JACK, MOLLIE, MISS PETTIGREW, MRS. DE LACY, SALLIE LONG, JIM DALY *and* HONOR BEWLEY. JACK (HUGH'*s brother*) *is an ordinary, stocky, cheerful young man.  His wife* MOLLIE *is a pretty ordinary young woman, rather swaggering in the fact that she is going to have a baby at the first legitimate moment.* MISS PETTIGREW *is quite old and dressed almost fantastically in a semi-evening dress of thirty years ago; her sister,* MRS. DE LACY, *is a little older, but very quietly and decently dressed in black.* SALLIE LONG *is a charming girl of twenty-two or twenty-three.* JIM DALY *is an odd, clever-looking fellow of twenty-six or twenty-seven.* HONOR BEWLEY *is about the same age, dressed in a simple black dress. All come in awkwardly, in a bunch, and having got in don't quite know what to do with themselves. The scene which follows must be so well produced that it gives the impression of not having been produced at all. People must move when they should not, mask each other, speak through each other's speeches—and yet every speech must be heard — the audience should say to each other, "What bad acting, what rotten production".)*

JACK. The whole bunch of us met on the doorstep, Mother. Hello, Hugh, back again; fine to see you.

HUGH (*shaking hands*). How are you, Jack?

JACK. Meet your new sister-in-law. Come here, Mollie. Where at all have you got to?

MOLLIE (*extricating herself from the little crowd*). Here I am. How-do-you-do, Hugh? I suppose I can call you that.

HUGH. Of course. I'm delighted to meet you at last.

MOLLIE. Yes, you were a swine not to come over to give Jack away.

HUGH. I had a play——

(*His sentence is drowned by* MRS. RIOR-
DAN's *greetings*.)

MRS. RIORDAN. How are you, Mrs. de
Lacy? You're looking frozen. Come near
the fire. Oh, and what a pretty dress, Sarah.
(*This to* MISS PETTIGREW.)

MISS PETTIGREW. Such an old rag.

MRS. RIORDAN. I don't believe it. It looks
the latest thing.

JACK (*to* HUGH). Well, you'll have to come
over for the christening—or stay over for it.
Won't he, Mollie?

HUGH. Christening?

JACK. You're to be godfather. We fixed
that, didn't we, Mollie, and if it's a boy we're
going to call it Hugh, after the genius of the
family.

MOLLIE. And if it's a girl—Moll——

JACK. After the demon of the family.

MRS. RIORDAN. Jack, please! Hugh, you
haven't forgotten Miss Pettigrew?

HUGH (*shaking hands*). Of course not.

MISS PETTIGREW (*simpering*). Indeed, I don't
know why you should remember—— Such
an old woman now. Years and years. And
this is my sister—Lucy!

MRS. DE LACY (*approaching*). You wanted
me, Sarah?

MISS PETTIGREW. This is Hugh. My sister,
Mrs. de Lacy.

HUGH. How-do-you-do? (MRS. DE LACY *bows*.)

MISS PETTIGREW. I don't think you've seen her since she was a child—no, I mean since you were a teeny, weeny child with the loveliest curls I ever saw.  She married into Carlow, you know, and then the beet came and her husband died and——

MRS. DE LACY. I'm sure, Sarah, Mr. Hugh doesn't want to hear all that.  You were in your pram when I saw you last.  You *have* grown.

HUGH. Yes, I suppose I have.

MRS. DE LACY. I remember you distinctly, but I do *not* remember any curls.  My recollection is that you were entirely bald.

MISS PETTIGREW. Oh, not bald, Lucy. Fluff. Down.

MRS. DE LACY. Bald.

HUGH. Probably.

MRS. RIORDAN (*bringing* SALLIE *forward*). And here is Miss Long.  She's a new-comer, the rector's daughter.

HUGH. How-do-you-do?

SALLIE. How-do-you-do?

MISS PETTIGREW. Such a nice man, Hugh, only been in the town for a year.  Came from somewhere near Lismore, didn't he, Sallie?

SALLIE. Yes, Miss Pettigrew.

MRS. DE LACY. On our honeymoon my husband and I *did* the valley of the Blackwater.

SALLIE. Really?

HUGH. Charming.

MISS PETTIGREW. I've always heard that Lismore Castle——

> (*Their conversation is lost for a moment; it is presumably about scenery and the Duke of Devonshire. Above the other conversation* AUNT MOLL'S *voice is heard; she is talking to* JIM DALY.)

AUNT MOLL. No, James Daly, there is no use in your trying to ram down my throat the fact that you are a medical student in your last year—almost a doctor. I do not approve of inoculation. I stand where I have always stood, right beside Mr. George Bernard Shaw.

JIM. Lucky George! But the statistics——

AUNT MOLL. Prove nothing. Or anything you want them to prove. Don't talk to me of your statistics. Come up to my room.

JIM. No, really!

HONOR. You ought to. Aunt Moll's room is a treasure-house.

MRS. RIORDAN. Come here, Jim. You and Hugh used to be great chums before you went to the National.

JIM (*going to* HUGH *and shaking hands*). Hallo, old man.

HUGH. Hallo, Jim. Nice to see you again.

JIM. I read about you in the papers from time to time. You're quite a person in literary London, aren't you? Makes me feel cocky to think that we were both at Rockwell together.

HUGH. Cocky? Rot. I'm a bloody failure. It's you that are getting the gold medals.

MRS. RIORDAN. Now you've met everyone, I think. Oh no, there's Honor hiding in the background. You don't need any introduction to *her*.

HUGH. No indeed. (*He crosses to meet her and shakes hands with her. There is a forced brightness and cordiality in his manner.*) How are you, Honor?

HONOR (*quite friendly and composed*). How-do-you-do, Hugh? It's nice for your mother to have you back.

HUGH. Oh yes.

HONOR. I was reading about your play. It was such a shame it wasn't more successful, it sounded so interesting. Of course I don't know anything about those sort of people but——

(*The rest of the conversation fades because* AUNT MOLL *tops it; she is talking to* MOLLIE.)

AUNT MOLL. I hope you take a good rest every afternoon. That's a very important thing. *I* know.

JACK (*laughing*). How could you know, Aunt Moll?

AUNT MOLL. I do. And another thing—James Daly, come here. Although I thoroughly disapprove of your views on inoculation and vivisection I think that you and I could tell this young woman that if she wants—no, don't run away—(*she pursues her to a corner of the room and captures her*).

HUGH (*to* HONOR). I was so sorry to hear of your bereavement. I meant to have written, but you know how it is.

HONOR. Poor father. He suffered so much. It was what is called a "blessed release".

HUGH (*always speaking with a little restraint*). You have your nice house still? You're going to stay on there?

HONOR. It's being auctioned next week.

HUGH. Oh, I say! You don't mean that— that he left you——?

HONOR. He left me plenty of money and that lovely old house.

HUGH. Then—then why?

(*Before she can answer* MISS PETTIGREW *is at* HUGH's *elbow*.)

MISS PETTIGREW. We hear you've had a play on the boards in London and that it was a tremendous success.

HUGH. It ran a week *and* two matinees.

MISS PETTIGREW. Isn't that magnificent? The one the Temperance Society put on at the Town Hall only ran two nights, though it was very good, I believe. Of course I couldn't go, my sister still being in mourning; only two years since Bob, my brother-in-law, died; a moving clot they said it was, very sad for all concerned. Of course I know that nowadays people go out of mourning faster than they go into it, but we're old-fashioned people, my sister and I, and——

MRS. DE LACY. Sarah!

MISS PETTIGREW. Am I talking too much, Lucy?

MRS. DE LACY. You are.

MISS PETTIGREW. I always was a bit of a rattle-tongue.

MRS. DE LACY. You were.

MISS PETTIGREW. You're always so grim with me, Lucy.

HONOR. You've the kindest tongue and the kindest heart in the town, Miss Pettigrew.

MISS PETTIGREW. Have I, dear? Thank you. And you've the prettiest face.

MRS. RIORDAN (*taking the floor*). I think we should go into tea at once and not wait for Mr. Riordan.

HONOR. Where is he, Mrs. Riordan?

MRS. RIORDAN. He's playing golf.

JACK. Playing in the Captain's prize; he's bound to be late.

AUNT MOLL. The Captain's prize! We all know what that means.

SALLIE LONG. Daddie's playing too.

AUNT MOLL. Oh, your father's all right. Band of Hope. But that nineteenth hole——!

JIM. You know everything, Miss Riordan.

AUNT MOLL. I don't play golf, thank God, but I'm not a fool. (*To* MOLLIE) I hear you've made Jack give up his golf?

MOLLIE. Yes, he gardens instead.

AUNT MOLL. Splendid. That bending. So good for the liver.

MOLLIE. And he's taken up his singing again.

JACK. I really only married her because I thought she might be able to play my accompaniments.

MOLLIE. Quite so, my dear.

AUNT MOLL. Jack had the makings of a good voice. (*She turns to him with perhaps the first touch of softness she has shown.*) Will you sing to me to-night, me dear? Nothing very old and nothing very new, just something seventyish or eightyish—like meself.

JACK (*taking a small pile of songs from the piano where he has laid them down when he came in*). I don't know if there's anything here you'd like. There are piles of others in the press.

AUNT MOLL (*turning them over*). "Bois Epais" —too smug and dreary. "The Erl-king"— you haven't guts enough to sing that properly. "So we'll go no more a-roving." Where did you get that?

JACK. It's an old song now, but still quite well known and a fine song. The music is by Maude Valerie White.

AUNT MOLL. I don't know it. I only know the poem, the most heartbreaking he ever wrote.

JACK. Who wrote? I never looked at the author of the words.

AUNT MOLL. Of course you didn't.  He was called George Gordon Byron.

JACK. Oh—Byron?  Did I learn him at school?

AUNT MOLL. It doesn't matter—for all the good it seems to have done you.  How does it go?  Hum it to me.

JACK. (*He sings very softly into her ear, so that it doesn't disturb the conversation in the room.*)

> So, we'll go no more a-roving
>> So late into the night,
> Though the heart——
>> (MR. RIORDAN *comes in.  Middle-aged, genial.  Plus-fours.*)

RIORDAN. Hallo, everyone.

MRS. RIORDAN. We were just giving you up, Joseph.  (*She rings a bell.*)

RIORDAN. I'm not so late.  Playing in the Captain's prize, you know.  I tied for second place.  That damned parson won.—Oh, beg pardon, Miss Long, didn't see you, but you know that your father and I are the best of friends; damned decent fellow.  Hallo, Hugh. Sorry couldn't get to the station to meet you, but Captain's prize, you know, couldn't be missed.  How's London and all that?  Gaiety girls, ha-ha!  Ah, Mrs. de Lacy, I've a little letter for you downstairs in the office—don't let me let you go without giving it to you; and there's your sister looking as pretty as a picture—you should have been my little mascot to-day, waved

success to me from the pavilion; and Honor—
you look half a nun already, bless you, my dear;
and there's my old witch of an aunt with her
broomstick parked in the landing—and Jim—
your father wasn't out this afternoon, scratched
at the last minute.

JIM. He's not feeling too fit—a touch of flu.

(RIORDAN *is only a little tipsy, and everyone
on his journey round the room has met
him very kindly and more than half-way.*)

MRS. RIORDAN. I've rung for tea.

RIORDAN. Good. I'm as hungry as a
hunter.

AUNT MOLL (*ominously*). Not *thirsty*, I expect.

RIORDAN. No, not thirst—yes, *very* thirsty.

AUNT MOLL. Humph!

MRS. RIORDAN. Well, by the time we're
sitting down Maggie will have the tea and
coffee up, so come along everyone. It's the
simplest sort of cold supper——

(*Babbling other courteous words she shoos
them to the door on the left.* HUGH
*hangs back and* AUNT MOLL *doesn't
move.*)

MRS. RIORDAN. Hugh, aren't you coming?

HUGH. Give me just a minute to finish this
cigarette.

MRS. RIORDAN. Well, don't be long.

MISS PETTIGREW (*as she goes out*). You're our
lion to-night, you know.

AUNT MOLL. Send me in me milk and biscuits, Kate. I couldn't bear to go in there and see you all gulping blancmange.

MRS. RIORDAN. Very well, Aunt Moll.

(*They all go into the next room except* HUGH *and* AUNT MOLL.)

AUNT MOLL. She'll forget, oh, she'll forget, she never remembers anything for more than five seconds. Oh well, Aunt Moll has the use of her own legs still, thank God; she can fetch her own milk and biscuits. A kind, feckless woman, that's what Kate is. She wouldn't even quench some of the lights. All that Shannon business has just led to extravagance and waste. Shannon scheme—oh, "scheme" is the word. (*She puts out all the lights except a bracket at the fireplace.*) That's enough light for you to smoke by, and it's enough light for me to read by while I sup me glass of milk.

HUGH. Yes. . . . (*Standing in front of the fire and waving his hand towards the door through which the company has disappeared.*) Well, there you are.

AUNT MOLL. How do you mean "There I are"?

HUGH. There's Knock for you. There's your comedy and tragedy—what was your ornamental phrase?—"trailing their skirts through the mud of Church Street". (*He laughs.*)

AUNT MOLL. There *you* are—if you only had the eyes to see it.

HUGH. I see them.

AUNT MOLL. You don't.

HUGH. I grant you they're all nice decent people.

AUNT MOLL (*with contempt*). Nice decent people!

HUGH. Do you mean to say they're not all nice and decent?

AUNT MOLL (*quietly and seriously*). I tell you, Hugh, there's a mort of tragedy and comedy sitting round that table in the next room—more tragedy than comedy I'm sorry to say.

HUGH. You're joking.

AUNT MOLL. I wish I was.

HUGH. What's tragic about any of them— except their awful provincialism?

AUNT MOLL. There are three plays for you there, maybe four, if you only had the guts to feel them and the eyes to see them.

HUGH. Plays? Ah, go on! I don't believe you for a minute.

AUNT MOLL (*thoughtful, not dictating*). Of course you'd have to select, choose what you'd take and what you'd leave aside. Didn't some-one say that genius was the art of selection? And you're no genius. You'd have to—sort of shape your material, just a little, a very little would be enough. Maybe you couldn't— maybe no dramatist could make that company inside into a play. Maybe it's only through the cinema you could catch it all, all the different stories, interlocking, moving away from each other, moving back to each other again, like figures in the lancers.

HUGH. Lancers?

AUNT MOLL. Maybe you're too young to have ever danced them. A figure dance, rowdy in a drawing-room, I've seen them danced in a kitchen in County Limerick, as dignified as an eighteenth-century minuet.

HUGH. Mother's party to-night seemed just a huddle of people, talking together anyhow and all getting in each other's way.

AUNT MOLL. I know. No construction. No stage-management. But, God Almighty, boy, that's your job.

HUGH. My job?

AUNT MOLL. As a dramatist. To put some shape, some stage-shape, on real life.

HUGH. Maybe. If there was only a subject there.

AUNT MOLL. I've told you. You have your choice of three or four.

HUGH. And I can't see even one.

AUNT MOLL. They tell me you're good at comedy, and I'm afraid there's not much comedy there——

HUGH. Oh come! Old Pettigrew and her sister.

AUNT MOLL. Hm, yes. But not as funny as they seem. There's your brother Jack and his wife—you'd better keep them in for the sake of normality, though it's a bit ironic that Jack, who was such a boyo, should be spancelled and tamed by that Mollie girl. Making him give up golf and take to gardening! Jack, who'd only recognise cabbage when it's boiled round a pig's head! Ha, ha! Oh, they're all right. They'll have a string of children, and Jack will die contentedly in his bed, aged eighty.

HUGH. You see; no play there.

AUNT MOLL. There's your father and mother——

HUGH. Normal again. The nicest people in the world, but utterly normal.

AUNT MOLL. Well, your father does take a drop too much now and again. I thought to-night he was distinctly elevated.

HUGH. Nonsense. And even if he was—the Captain's match. I have seen him tipsy but not enough to make a song and dance about it, and if you think I'm going to put my own father on the stage and show him drunk——

AUNT MOLL. Charles Dickens put his father in a book and didn't show him up so well. But no; I suppose we'll have to leave Joseph out, he doesn't get raging drunk, and, of course, poor Kate's a rock of morality—did she send me in me milk?

HUGH. No. Don't mind it for a minute. I'll get it. Go on. This is beginning to interest me.

AUNT MOLL. You ought to make yourself the villain of the play.

HUGH. I? What, under heaven, have I done?

AUNT MOLL. You, and Honor Bewley.

HUGH. Honor?

AUNT MOLL. Don't pretend to be so surprised. You broke her heart.

HUGH. I don't believe it.

AUNT MOLL. You did, when you went off to London seven years ago and left her behind.

HUGH. Nonsense. We were never engaged. There was nothing between us.

AUNT MOLL. There was everything between you except the one word "Honor, will you marry me?" Do you remember how gay she was long ago, and look at her now. That's what your seven years' desertion has done.

HUGH. I have nothing to do with her looks. She's had a hard time, nursing her paralysed father. That aged her, naturally.

AUNT MOLL. If she'd been married to you, she'd have thrown over her father, paralysed and all as he was. What is it Mr. Shaw says? "Girls withering into ladies." Oh, but Honor Bewley's the withered lady.

HUGH. I don't believe you for a minute. She met me to-night without a flicker of embarrassment, she was icily calm.

AUNT MOLL. Don't you know why? . . . Ah, use your imagination, man. Don't you know what it's in her head to do?

HUGH. No. . . . (*Something dawns on him.*) I don't want to know. I mean—I mean——

AUNT MOLL. You're afraid.

HUGH (*shaking it off*). Oh, let's fish round somewhere else. Let's be gay, macabre if you like. What about old Pettigrew and her monumental sister?

AUNT MOLL. Yes, make them as monumental as you like, but don't forget that there's something behind Sarah Pettigrew's gazebo of a dress.

HUGH (*laughing*). A broken heart?

AUNT MOLL. No. An empty stomach.

HUGH (*sobered*). Oh!

AUNT MOLL. I don't know for certain, Hugh, but I believe that those two women are hungry half the time. You know, apart from the big old house they have rent-free for the rest of their lives, they never had much money in their pockets; but they were the most generous creatures in the world—at least Sarah was; we don't know so much about the Lucy one. No beggar was ever turned from their door without a square meal and a shilling in his pocket. Well, now I hear there's neither bread nor a shilling for the decentest tinker walking the roads. I think they were living on the bit that came from the railways or some investments of the sort, but since they've failed—well, your father would know, he handles their investments, but of course I couldn't ask him.

There's something to catch hold of there, Hugh.

HUGH. By Jove, yes. But it can't be true.

AUNT MOLL. People are hungry, Hugh, even in Knock, not only on the London Embankment. Didn't you notice the sort of grey look on their faces?

HUGH. No.

AUNT MOLL. That's what I'm telling you. You've no eyes, no imagination.

HUGH. I'll look closer next time. Well, who'd think that my oddities should turn out to be half-tragic figures? But when I write my play I'll keep them in for a kind of macabre relief. I'll have to get my nice fun, my romance, out of Jim Daly and Miss—I forget her name, but they seemed a bit gone on each other.

AUNT MOLL. Sallie Long. The rector's daughter.

HUGH. Oh yes. So she was.

AUNT MOLL. The rector's daughter and Jim Daly—in love with one another. Doesn't that suggest something to you?

HUGH. I don't think so.

AUNT MOLL. Don't you remember how great Jim's people always were with the Church? One uncle a Monsignor and the other a P.P. in Liverpool; two aunts nuns, and Jim himself, though he is a medical student, not wild at all, not likely to do anything rash, anything that would go against his family and his religion.

HUGH. You mean he'd like to marry her if she wasn't a Protestant?

AUNT MOLL. They're dying down about each other, and she won't go against *her* religion. We must give in, Hugh, that now and again Protestants are as hot on their faith as we are on ours. The thing is breaking their hearts.

HUGH. God!

AUNT MOLL. The whole town knows of it; I'm not making it up, 'tis the laugh of every public-house. Old Daly is threatening all sorts. Poor Mrs. Daly is just amiable, bewildered, the creature. What's to be the end of it, God alone knows.

HUGH. One or the other will give in.

AUNT MOLL. Neither will give in, they're both too proud. . . . I hear there's talk of her going to London.

HUGH. To forget him? I see. A good idea.

AUNT MOLL (*darkly*). Maybe.

HUGH. Maybe? If not for that reason, why?

AUNT MOLL. I don't know, and I wouldn't tell you if I did. . . . Well, there's bits of a play for you, Hugh.

HUGH. Yes, but only bits. I'd have to bring you in to bind it all together.

AUNT MOLL. Let you leave me out of it.

HUGH. Indeed I won't. What are you, Aunt Moll? Comedy or tragedy?

AUNT MOLL. Just a cantankerous old woman.

HUGH. Yes, of course. But something else.

AUNT MOLL. Melodrama.

HUGH. I don't believe it.

AUNT MOLL. I've shot me man.

HUGH. Aunt Moll! A *crime passionel?*

AUNT MOLL. Not at all. A Black-and-Tan.

HUGH. Good God! I think I'm going crazy.

AUNT MOLL. I shot him through the heart. Oh, none of your dirty shoot-him-in-the-back jobs for Aunty Moll. . . . There's a hat-box under me bed.

HUGH. What's in it?

AUNT MOLL (*with a chuckle*). A relic. Human.

HUGH. Merciful heavens! And you used to teach me my cathecism! (*He gets up; he is anywhere about the room; he is fearfully excited.*) You're right, you're right, there's a play here somewhere. I don't quite know where, I don't quite know with whom, I'll have to fish round, try here and there, get them back, not really back, I only mean back in my mind—and in yours, Aunt Moll, for you must help me. But I don't want everyone together, just two or three at a time. . . . I think I'm beginning to see it now . . . those starving old women . . . and Sallie Long and London . . . how frightful . . . how perfectly ghastly. . . . But it's inevitable—or is it? Is it all in my own mind or must it—must it happen? Am I shaping events or are they shaping me? Is it all pre-destined? (*He raises his voice and speaks with a harsh, unnatural note.*) Will you all stand by, please. I'll summon you as I need you. We'll sit over this side, Aunt Moll. I must see them on the stage as I see them in my mind. I'll alter the lights and arrange the furniture as I go along.

AUNT MOLL. Use your imagination, Hugh.

HUGH. I'll try to.

(*He switches off all the lights and in the darkness pilots her to the extreme left of the stage. They sit on two chairs, facing diagonally from lower left corner to upper right. A faint light comes up. The back wall of the room has dis-appeared and has been replaced by a wall somewhat similar to it but with a bench about four feet from the ground stretching across it, and on the bench are sitting all the characters we have seen earlier in the play with the exception of JACK and MOLLIE. They sit quite motionless, like dummy figures, we see them dimly.*)

HUGH (*surveying them*). Yes, that will do. . . . I don't think we need take it right from the beginning, Aunt Moll, I mean the bit about my coming down here and telling mother I'm not staying—oh but I say, I can't do myself, I've got to stage-manage, construct. Besides

I want to imagine a young man, much more attractive than I am . . . a little tragic-looking . . . yes, that's it.

> (*As if evoked, a young man is standing by the fire.*)

And now, Mother—you've gone out of the room by this time, Aunt Moll, to get your bally milk.

AUNT MOLL. I've told you, I don't want to be in the play at all.

HUGH. What a hope! Just you wait!

> (*During these two sentences* MRS. RIORDAN *has come from the bench and taken her place beside the Evoked* HUGH. *The scenes which follow with the evoked characters should, if possible, be a little different in production from the scenes with the natural characters, the speeches a little slower and more deliberate, the movements slightly stagey.*)

EV. HUGH. No, I'm not staying.

MRS. RIORDAN. Not staying?

EV. HUGH. Just till to-morrow morning.

MRS. RIORDAN. But why? You've only just come. Is it a new play? Is that why you've got to rush back to London?

EV. HUGH. No.

MRS. RIORDAN. Then what is it? Oh, Hugh, I've looked forward to this visit of yours for so long.

EV. HUGH. I know, but——

REAL HUGH. I'll break it there.    Honor!

EV. HUGH. I know, but——

MRS. RIORDAN. Hush.    Someone's arrived. Don't make up your mind yet, Hugh, we'll talk of it later.

REAL HUGH. And now for Honor.

> (HONOR BEWLEY *has got off the bench and comes in through the door.*)

MRS. RIORDAN. Ah, how are you, my dear?

HONOR (*shaking hands*). Am I the first?

MRS. RIORDAN. Yes, but what matter?  You can have a nice chat with Hugh before all the others arrive.

HONOR. How do you do, Hugh?

EV. HUGH (*meeting her awkwardly*). How are you, Honor?

HONOR. It's quite a long time since we've seen you.

EV. HUGH. Four years.

MRS. RIORDAN. Will you excuse me, Honor dear, if I just slip into the dining-room and have a look at the supper-table?    Maggie's as good as gold, but forgetful.

> (*She goes out.*)

HONOR (*smiling*). Your mother was always diplomatic.

EV. HUGH. I was so sorry to hear of your bereavement.    I meant to have written—but you know how it is.

HONOR. Of course.    You were so busy with your writing.    I quite understood.

EV. HUGH. You're looking—— (*He pauses for a word.*)

HONOR. Older? Tired?

EV. HUGH. Well—grave. Very grave.

HONOR. I'll try not to be at your party. I'm sure I am looking old and tired, but father's was such a long illness and I nursed him myself. He suffered so much, his death was what is called a "blessed release".

EV. HUGH. Mother told me that he left you quite well off and you still have the nice house. You'll live on there, of course?

HONOR. It's being auctioned next week.

EV. HUGH. Honor! Why?

HONOR. Oh, I have other plans.

EV. HUGH (*laughing*). I believe you're going to get married.

HONOR (*pained*). Hugh!

EV. HUGH. I shouldn't have said that. I'm sorry.

HONOR. It doesn't matter. . . . Listen, Hugh, after the next few days I shall never see you again.

EV. HUGH. Honor!

HONOR. Never again. So for your sake— for both our sakes—I want to say something to you quite frankly. You remember I had barely met you till I was over seventeen. I was away at school or you were away at school. I was a very religious girl; I wanted to be a nun; I thought I had a vocation, I still think I had a

vocation, and father didn't object and then—
and then——

EV. HUGH. And then I came along.

HONOR. Exactly. You came along. It was
fun for you those long summer holidays and the
Christmas after.

EV. HUGH. I loved you very much, Honor, I
did indeed.

HONOR. I know you thought you did; but
when there was a question of your going to
London and being very poor and having to
make your own way——

EV. HUGH. I couldn't bear the idea of being
spancelled and strangled by an engagement of
marriage. I couldn't, Honor, I couldn't. That
evening, walking home from the dance at the
Bank—do you remember?—(*she nods*), I was
going to London the next day, it was on the tip
of my tongue to ask you to marry me, and I
just managed not to; and I came home and threw
myself on my bed and said, "I'm free, I'm free,
thank God, I'm still free."

HONOR. I was free too, but I didn't want to
be free. And you hardly ever wrote, so I knew
it was all over. And then I set myself to forget
you, and it took me a few years, but I succeeded
at last; and now you are less to me than any
stranger I might pass in the street. I suppose
you "broke my heart" as they used to say, but it's
mended again; and now that father's dead I'm free
to do what I should have done after I left school.

EV. HUGH. You mean—become a nun?

HONOR. Yes.

EV. HUGH. You make me feel an awful brute.

HONOR. You needn't feel that.   I think you should never forget the rather mean way you treated me;  but maybe it was for the best, for if I had been a nun I couldn't have looked after poor father.   Anyway, all's over now, Hugh, and let's shake hands quickly as old friends before the others come in.   (*She holds out her hand.*)

EV. HUGH. Honor, perhaps even still——

HONOR. Nonsense.   You're quite out of my heart.   God bless you, Hugh;  may you be as happy as I shall be.   (*She shakes his hand warmly.*)

> (MR. RIORDAN *comes in;  he has been drinking, and it makes him excited and brusque.*)

MR. RIORDAN. Hallo.   What are you two colloguing about?   Sorry, Honor.   I should have shaken hands with you, but I'm a bit put out this evening.   What do you think of this fine lad of mine?

HONOR. I think he's looking very well, Mr. Riordan.

MR. RIORDAN. Yes, why shouldn't he?   Living on the fat of the land in London.   Wish I had the chance of getting away for a bit.

HONOR. You have been looking pulled down for the last couple of months.

MR. RIORDAN. Nonsense. Never better, never better. Where's your mother, Hugh? I must see Kate. Business. I've to telephone to Dublin at once.

HONOR. I'll get her, Mr. Riordan, she's in the dining-room, I think.

EV. HUGH. No, let me go.

HONOR. Don't bother.

MR. RIORDAN. Yes, both of you go if you don't mind. It's a little bit of private business —nothing important you know, but private.

(EV. HUGH *opens the door for* HONOR *and she goes out.* EV. HUGH *gives his father a searching look.*)

MR. RIORDAN (*resenting it*). You think I've been drinking? Well, I have, and so would you if you were in my shoes.

EV. HUGH. I'm sorry. Can I do anything— help in any way?

MR. RIORDAN. No, you can't. But thanks all the same.

(EV. HUGH *goes out.*)

AUNT MOLL. I don't like this, Hugh. Joseph isn't a bad boy.

HUGH. Hush, Aunt Moll. Remember it's half play-acting.

(MRS. RIORDAN *comes in.*)

MRS. RIORDAN. You wanted me, Joseph?

MR. RIORDAN. Yes. You know those Blenkinsop shares you have?

MRS. RIORDAN. Blenkinsop?

134

MR. RIORDAN. Yes; Blenkinsop, Blenkinsop.
I want you to lend them to me; I must raise some
money on them at once.

MRS. RIORDAN. Oh.

MR. RIORDAN. I'll be able to give them back
to you in a couple of months.

(MRS. RIORDAN *says nothing.*)
You trust me, don't you? You don't think
I'm going to make away with them?

MRS. RIORDAN. Of course not. But—but
I haven't got them.

MR. RIORDAN. Not got them?

MRS. RIORDAN. I sold them, three months
ago.

MR. RIORDAN. Behind my back, without
telling me a word?

MRS. RIORDAN. Yes, Joseph.

MR. RIORDAN. In the name of Heaven, why?
What have you been doing?

MRS. RIORDAN. Nothing wrong, Joseph, but
I knew you'd be angry. It was for Hugh.

MR. RIORDAN. Hugh? What did he want
money for? Hadn't he his allowance? Debts?

MRS. RIORDAN. No, it was money for his
play. He could only get it on by putting some
money into it himself and, of course, he
hadn't a penny beyond his little allowance.
(MR. RIORDAN *sits down, collapsed.*) You're not
angry with me, Joseph?

MR. RIORDAN. No, I'm not angry, I'm
beyond that.

MRS. RIORDAN. You're frightening me. What's happened?

MR. RIORDAN. I've been a blasted fool, Kate. I've been worse. A criminal. I've been gambling with other people's money.

MRS. RIORDAN. Joseph!

MR. RIORDAN. Miss Pettigrew's and her sister's, of all unfortunate people. I thought I could double their money for them—no, I didn't really do it for their sakes; if I'd doubled it I'd have kept the makings for myself—and now, unless I can find three hundred pounds by to-morrow morning it's all gone.

MRS. RIORDAN. Ah, the poor women!

MR. RIORDAN. They won't starve, I won't let them starve anyway. Oh, my God, what a fool I've been, what a blasted fool.

MRS. RIORDAN. I've thirty or more pounds in the bank, Joseph.

MR. RIORDAN. Yes, I'll use that to go on with, and then I'll think of some way—there must be some way.

(JIM *and* SALLIE *come in, there are mutual greetings.*)

MR. RIORDAN (*irritably*). Are we all here? Can't we have supper now, Kate. I'm starving.

MRS. RIORDAN. I'm expecting a couple more, dear.

MR. RIORDAN. Who?

MRS. RIORDAN. Miss—Miss Pettigrew and Mrs. de Lacy.

MR. RIORDAN. Oh, my God!

JIM. You say that as if you didn't like them, as if you weren't their best friend—which they always swear you are.

SALLIE. Friend? Why, Jim—you've been away in Dublin, but if you could see the way Mr. Riordan flirts with Miss Pettigrew at the badminton, it's—it's quite shameless. I wonder you allow it, Mrs. Riordan.

MRS. RIORDAN (*trying to smile*). I know, dear. Shocking, isn't it? But—you're not looking quite yourself. Are you feeling quite well?

SALLIE (*quickly, brazening it out*). Never felt fitter, Mrs. Riordan. Running round a little too much perhaps.

MRS. RIORDAN. You should take care of yourself. (*Taking in* JIM *with her eyes.*) Ah yes, of course.

MR. RIORDAN (*slapping* JIM *on the back*). Young people will be young people.

JIM (*uncomfortable*). Yes, yes. Playing golf to-day, Mr. Riordan?

MR. RIORDAN. No, Jim. Too busy, too busy. I forgot, aren't Jack and Mollie coming?

MRS. RIORDAN. Not till after supper, Joseph.
(*The door opens and* HUGH *admits* MISS PETTIGREW *and her sister.*)

MISS PETTIGREW. We met Mr. Hugh in the hall—how do you do, Mrs. Riordan? My sister says he's grown. Sallie, my dear (*she kisses her*), and Jim, of course, never very far away, ha, ha! And there's Mr. Riordan hiding from me, positively hiding from me. I see you, you naughty man; come here and shake hands with me. (*He comes forward unwillingly.*) Hold up your head! I believe Kate has been giving you a good dressing-down, and I'm sure you deserved it. Have you, Kate?

(MRS. DE LACY *meanwhile is making proper salutations.*)

MRS. RIORDAN. No, oh no.

MISS PETTIGREW. Of course you couldn't. None of us could have the heart to do anything or say anything against dear Mr. Riordan, our best friend, our oldest friend.

(HONOR *opens the dining-room door.*)

HONOR. Supper's ready now, Mrs. Riordan.

MRS. RIORDAN. Thank you, dear. Come along everyone. (*And, talking easily and moving easily, they all go into the dining-room and the door is shut.*)

AUNT MOLL. And that, I suppose, properly worked up, is your first act?

HUGH. I'm not sure. I'd like to run the play straight through in a series of little scenes.

AUNT MOLL. Taking how long?

HUGH. Maybe an hour, maybe an hour and a half.

AUNT MOLL. Nonsense. No audience would stand it. Not an audience of men anyway.

Never can sit for more than half an hour without wanting a smoke or a drink or—or something. No self-control.

HUGH. They stick it at the pictures. I'll try them anyway. The fact is, Aunt Moll, you've no self-control; you are dying for your milk.

AUNT MOLL. Of course I am. It's beyond me hour.

HUGH (*going towards the dining-room door*). I'll get it for you.

AUNT MOLL (*calling after him*). And me Marie biscuits.

HUGH (*disappearing*). You'll get them.

AUNT MOLL. The creature. His mother all over. Feckless. I'll warrant he'll forget the biscuits—or the milk, no system, no imagination. Ah well, I've me *Manchester Guardian*. (*She picks up the paper but before she has time to start to read it* HUGH *is back with a glass of milk, two Marie biscuits, and a glass of claret.*)

HUGH. Here's your milk, Aunt Moll, *and* your biscuits.

AUNT MOLL. Thank you. (*She has a good gulp of milk.*)

HUGH (*after a sip of claret*). I know I should have used them more, those two old women for queerities' sake. I could do them as easily as I—as I—but they're all there, in my mind. I can plug them in later on if it's necessary. Just now, just for a first draft I wanted to bring them in bare and neat—like a very dry sherry. But don't fret, Aunt Moll, I'll enrich it all later. What I want you to do now is run upstairs and get into a mackintosh and a very plain hat.

AUNT MOLL. I certainly will do nothing of the kind. At this hour of night!

HUGH. Oh yes, you will. Don't you understand, I'm master here this evening. Whatever I say, goes. I clap my hands, presto!— and you disappear.

AUNT MOLL (*going*). Well, I never!

(*She goes out.*)

(*There is a sound of ping-pong balls from the dining-room, sound of people scoring and laughter. The door opens and* SALLIE LONG *comes in. She moves to the fire and stands there rather wearily. A few seconds later* JIM DALY *comes after her.*)

JIM. You slipped away. Why did you? We were all so jolly.

SALLIE. Yes, you were.

JIM. Don't you like table-tennis—ping-pong or whatever they call it?

SALLIE. I used to.

JIM. Why wouldn't you play this evening?

SALLIE. Aren't you almost a doctor?

JIM. Yes. . . . I forgot, for a minute.

SALLIE. Go back to the others. They'll miss you.

JIM. They won't.   I've been knocked out.

SALLIE. Still, they'll miss you.

JIM. Look here, Sallie, things can't go on like this.

SALLIE. Why not?

JIM. I'll marry you to-morrow, like a shot.

SALLIE. Yes.   On the old conditions.   Oh Jim, my dear, don't let's go over it all again. We've argued and argued.   There's no possible solution.

JIM. You can't bring yourself to do it?

SALLIE. Turn Catholic?   No.   Isn't it queer that I could let myself do with you—what I did, and yet I can't go back on my faith?   I could never bring myself to say that I believe in things I don't believe in, things that I hate in my heart.   You can't give up your faith either.   I respect you for it, respect me.

JIM. I do.   You'll always be the only woman——

SALLIE. Stop.   Don't make rash promises, and don't look so awfully solemn.   After all, isn't it a very old story—the medical student and the clergyman's daughter?   Aren't there vulgar jokes about it—or comic songs?

JIM. Oh, shut up.

SALLIE. When Jack and Mollie came in to-night there were mildly facetious jokes made about her "condition"—isn't that what it's called?   Everyone was as pleased as punch.

Suppose that I went into that room this minute and told them of *my* condition, what would they say?

JIM. You wouldn't.

SALLIE. Of course not. But suppose I did and said you were the father?

JIM. But what's going to happen?

SALLIE. I'm going to London next week.

JIM. To London?

SALLIE. Well, Jim, father's awfully broad-minded, but my having my bastard at the Rectory would be a little bit thick.

JIM. Who are you going to in London?

SALLIE. School friend.

JIM. I don't believe you.

SALLIE. Well, it's an easy thing to say.

JIM. I want your address.

SALLIE. Why? Don't you see it's all over, Jim? (*He starts to protest.*) Oh, very well, you shall have it, but I don't promise to write.

JIM. I'll write often.

SALLIE (*sure that he won't*). I'm sure you will. When do you go back to Dublin?

JIM. To-morrow morning.

SALLIE. Oh. . . . Then to-night is good-bye.

JIM. No, of course not.

SALLIE. Yes, it is. (*Quite lightly*) Good-bye, Jim.

JIM. You're horribly cruel.

SALLIE. I mean to be.

JIM. You're putting me in the wrong all the time.

SALLIE. I'm not, I'm not. Oh, forgive me, my dear and—there's one thing—thank your mother from me, somehow I can't, and tell her how sweet and nice she's been. I think she'd have liked me for a daughter-in-law—if things had only been different.

JIM. I'll tell her. Father's been a beast.

SALLIE. Ah no. Behaved just the way you'll behave to your children—your legitimate children. We'd better go back to the others, they'll be wondering.

JIM. Yes, come along.

(*As they are going* SALLIE *stops. She holds out her arms to him.*)

SALLIE. Jim, good-bye.

JIM (*kissing her passionately*). Oh, my dear, my dear.

SALLIE. My poor Jim.

(*They go into the next room. Hugh walks about the room slightly re-arranging the furniture and talking as he does so.*)

HUGH. A big dining-room in an old Georgian house; it's a sitting-room too, for of course they only use the drawing-room when they give a party and that they haven't done for years—Mrs. de Lacy's mourning makes such a convenient excuse. A few worthless old portraits on the walls, some good mahogany

furniture, gimcrack candlesticks on the fine
Adams mantelpiece, two pictures of comic cats
by Louis Wain. The light is cold and dim.
(*He does something to the light switches.*) Yes,
like that.

> (MISS PETTIGREW (SARAH) *and* MRS. DE
> LACY (LUCY) *come in, taking off their
> wraps, showing themselves in the
> dresses we saw them in at the party.
> They sit beside the fire.*)

MISS PETTIGREW. Look, Lucy, fancy! The
fire is still in.

MRS. DE LACY. So it is.

MISS PETTIGREW. Those beech logs are
wonderful, they last so long. Why it's nearly
three hours since we left for the Riordans.
Shall I put another log on?

MRS. DE LACY. Better go to bed. There are
only two logs left in the basket, you'll have to
cut some more to-morrow.

MISS PETTIGREW. Yes, indeed I will.

MRS. DE LACY. I wish I could help you, but
—my heart.

MISS PETTIGREW. Of course, Lucy. And I
don't mind cutting logs a bit, it's warming
work. I always say that about logs, they
warm you while you're making them and they
warm you when they're burning.

MRS. DE LACY. I wish to goodness you
wouldn't be for ever looking on the bright
side of things, Sarah, it's—it's most irritating.

MISS PETTIGREW. Is it, Lucy? I'm sorry but I can't help feeling gay to-night after that lovely party. (*She starts to hum "So, we'll go no more a-roving".*)

MRS. DE LACY. Do be quiet. You were ridiculous to-night. You were as gay as—as a three-year-old.

MISS PETTIGREW. Was I, Lucy? Did I chatter too much?

MRS. DE LACY. You did?

MISS PETTIGREW. Isn't that dreadful of me? But the lights, and all the young people, and the lovely food, and that mulled claret—they went to my head I suppose.

> (*She gets up and starts to waltz, singing.*)
> So, we'll go no more a-roving
>    So late into the night.

MRS. DE LACY. Sit down and behave yourself.

MISS PETTIGREW (*still dancing*). No, join me, partner me. You always used to be gentleman when we practised dancing long ago together. Come on, Lucy.

MRS. DE LACY. Ridiculous. At our age.

MISS PETTIGREW (*waltzing to her*). Come on.
> (*She pulls her up. Far away a ghostly piano and violin are heard playing the waltz from "The Merry Widow".*)

MISS PETTIGREW. That was the waltz they played—do you remember?—at the Hunt Ball the night Bob proposed to you.

MRS. DE LACY. I remember.

MISS PETTIGREW. Mr. Clarke-Barry's band, wasn't it? We had met Mr. de Lacy at the Dublin Exhibition. That was nineteen hundred and seven, wasn't it, Lucy?

MRS. DE LACY. Yes. The Morgans introduced us.

MISS PETTIGREW. How happy you were that evening after the ball. You came into my room; we brushed each other's hair, and you told me about Bob.

MRS. DE LACY. I remember.

MISS PETTIGREW. We were both so happy. Bob was so handsome.

MRS. DE LACY. But no good as a husband. You were luckier, Sarah, after all.

MISS PETTIGREW. Because I never loved anyone? Or at least no one ever loved me. Was I, Lucy?

MRS. DE LACY. Of course you were.

MISS PETTIGREW. I don't know. When I saw those young people to-night—Jack and Mollie and Mr. Daly and Miss Long—I felt I could almost cry.

MRS. DE LACY. Nonsense. Jack and Mollie are the most ordinary people. Bob and I—I admit that Bob was hopeless as a business man and as a husband—but we were never ordinary.

MISS PETTIGREW. Maybe Mollie doesn't think Jack ordinary.

MRS. DE LACY. Rubbish. I won't dance any more. It's ridiculous, at our age.

*(They stop dancing.)*

MISS PETTIGREW. I danced three times to-night, with Mr. Riordan and Mr. Daly and Jack.

MRS. DE LACY. I saw you. Disgraceful.

MISS PETTIGREW. Was it? I'm sorry. But it was all so lovely. If only Hugh hadn't behaved so queerly. What was the matter with him, do you think?

MRS. DE LACY. Oh, just nerves and foolishness, I suppose. I'm sure he leads a most dissipated life in London; I'm told all young men there do.

MISS PETTIGREW. Kate always says he's the steadiest of boys.

MRS. DE LACY. Hm! . . . Read the papers. Murders. Suicides. Night-clubs. . . . By the way, what was he saying about your bag?

MISS PETTIGREW. My bag? Oh nothing. Just nonsense.

MRS. DE LACY. It sounded nonsense to me but you got so flustered I thought for a minute there must be something in it.

MISS PETTIGREW. In it? In the bag?

MRS. DE LACY. In what he was saying.

MISS PETTIGREW. Well—in a way—there was.

MRS. DE LACY. There was? What do you mean?

MISS PETTIGREW. You'll be cross with me, Lucy, I know, but I couldn't resist it, and no one saw me, I'll swear to that, and Hugh wasn't in the room at the time so I don't know how he suspected, and anyhow I didn't let him open my bag, and we haven't tasted butter for a week——

MRS. DE LACY. What on earth are you talking about?

MISS PETTIGREW. Those little rolls with the sausages inside them—weren't they lovely?

MRS. DE LACY. They were very nice. I only had one; I'd have liked another but the plate never came round again.

MISS PETTIGREW. It came round to me. And I thought—a couple of them for our breakfast——

MRS. DE LACY. Sarah!

MISS PETTIGREW. Yes. I slipped them into my bag, two of them.

MRS. DE LACY. You stole them?

MISS PETTIGREW. It wasn't exactly stealing, Lucy. Kate Riordan would strip her table for us and well you know it. But I couldn't ask her for food.

MRS. DE LACY. I should think not.

MISS PETTIGREW (*taking the rolls out of her bag*). Look, there they are. They smell so nice. . . . You're furious with me, Lucy?

MRS. DE LACY (*after a pause*). I should be, but I'm not. My God, that shows how low we've sunk.

MISS PETTIGREW. Things will be better in a little while when the hens begin to lay again.

MRS. DE LACY. To be depending on half a dozen hens! The Pettigrews to be waiting on six white Wyandottes. Thank God Papa never lived to see this day.

MISS PETTIGREW. They're very red in the comb, they'll be laying any day now. And we're never cold, Lucy, with all the old trees on the place. And I don't mind cutting up the logs, not a bit. There's others worse off than we are. (*Timidly*) Would you eat the roll now?

MRS. DE LACY. It would choke me.

MISS PETTIGREW. Indeed I don't feel hungry either. I'll heat them for the breakfast. That mulled claret—it warmed the cockles of the heart, didn't it, Lucy? I thought Mr. Riordan took a little too much whiskey before the evening was over. Did you think so, Lucy? Indeed one shouldn't say a word against him, he's such a kind man and has been the best of friends to us.

MRS. DE LACY. That reminds me—he gave me a letter when we were leaving.

MISS PETTIGREW. What was in it?

MRS. DE LACY. I hadn't a chance to read it.

MISS PETTIGREW. Maybe the shares are paying again.

MRS. DE LACY. Maybe they are. He said it might be years before we'd get a dividend, but that in the long run they were as safe as could be.

(*She takes a letter from her bag.*)

MISS PETTIGREW. Hurry and see what he says.

MRS. DE LACY (*opening the letter*). The light's dim. (*Reading*) "Dear Mrs. de Lacy—As an old friend of yours and of your sister's . . . not offended . . . sake of old times . . . well, well. . . .

MISS PETTIGREW. What is it?

MRS. DE LACY. He's sent a cheque, he's offering us money.

MISS PETTIGREW. Money?

MRS. DE LACY. Twenty pounds, to tide us over the winter, he says.

MISS PETTIGREW. Twenty pounds! Oh, isn't he the generous man?

MRS. DE LACY. Indeed he is.

MISS PETTIGREW. We could get a few clothes, and maybe a little goat, and we'd have milk for our tea and meal for the hens and—and——

MRS. DE LACY. We'd have nothing of the sort.

MISS PETTIGREW. Why not? What would you spend it on?

MRS. DE LACY. Good friend as Joseph Riordan is I'd die sooner than take anything from him. He's done his best for us, he's looked after our stocks and shares and 'tisn't his fault that all has gone wrong with us. If I took this money from him I could never walk into his house again and hold my head up.

MISS PETTIGREW. But you weren't cross with me for taking the rolls.

MRS. DE LACY. I should have been. Never

must you do such a thing again. Promise me, Sarah.

MISS PETTIGREW (*starting to cry*) I can't promise. I can't trust myself not to. You're strong, Lucy, I'm weak, I'm hungry. I want nice clothes, I want nice food. Don't I know that I look a fright going around in old Aunt Julia's clothes of thirty years ago. I make a joke about it and say I'm all in the fashion, but of course I'm not. I'm—I'm comic.

MRS. DE LACY. You're not. You're a lady whatever clothes you wear.

MISS PETTIGREW. I'm tired of being a lady, tired of this poverty, tired of trying to keep up an appearance and knowing that everyone sees through it, and that the men lounging outside the public-houses and seeing me pass talk of me as "poor ould Miss Pettigrew".

MRS. DE LACY. They don't. How do you know they do?

MISS PETTIGREW. I don't know for certain, but I just know.

MRS. DE LACY. If we're poor it's through no fault of our own.

MISS PETTIGREW. That makes no difference. Maybe they'd think more of us if we had lost it card-playing or horse-racing. Not that I care what they think. But, twenty pounds! Oh, however will you thank Joseph Riordan?

MRS. DE LACY. I'll write to him very nicely and tell him we're in no need.

MISS PETTIGREW. You'll send back the cheque?

MRS. DE LACY. Of course.

MISS PETTIGREW. You'll tell him we're in no need? That'll be a lie he won't easily believe.

MRS. DE LACY. He's gentleman enough to take it as it's meant to be taken, as a polite refusal of his help. After all, it isn't his fault that our shares have come to nothing.

MISS PETTIGREW. No. . . . But to send back all that money. . . . Lucy!

MRS. DE LACY. I won't send it back. I'll burn the cheque—now.

MISS PETTIGREW. No, no, please, Lucy, wait till the morning.

MRS. DE LACY. There's enough fire left to burn it.

MISS PETTIGREW. Wait till the morning. Maybe you'll think different in the morning.

MRS. DE LACY. That's what I'm afraid of, Sarah, I might think different in the morning. Isn't it queer the difference good food and a drop of wine make? I'm feeling very high and moral now, I mightn't feel so moral in the morning.

(*She burns the cheque.*)

MISS PETTIGREW (*in a little voice*). I'll burn the rolls if you like, Lucy.

MRS. DE LACY. No, no, child, keep them. Have the two of them for your breakfast.

MISS PETTIGREW. I couldn't eat them; they'd stick in my throat.

MRS. DE LACY. They'll do nothing of the sort. I'll share with you if that will help you. Maybe it will do my pride good to eat stolen food. (*Miss Pettigrew begins to cry.*) There, there, I didn't mean to start you crying. . . . I declare I believe I'm crying myself.

> (*She puts her arms round her sister and the scene fades.*)

HUGH (*moving about in the darkness as if he were arranging furniture, which he probably isn't*). A white bed here, an image of the Blessed Virgin, a little lamp, and Honor in her night-dress kneeling before it; she has said her prayers, she is going to bed.

> (*A light comes up and we see* HONOR *kneeling in her white night-dress.*)

HONOR. I thought I had utterly forgotten; I thought I had torn him entirely out of my heart. But I was deceiving myself and I was trying to deceive you, Holy Mother. This flower, this daisy he gave me long ago, I have kept it. Now I tear it to pieces. See! It's all gone, it's all forgotten. I'm empty now, empty of every human affection.

> (*She takes her Thomas à Kempis from the bed and reads.*)

"Lord, how oft shall I resign myself and wherein shall I forsake myself? . . . I have said to thee full oft and yet I say again; forsake thyself, resign of thyself and thou shalt enjoy great peace. To this enforce thyself, this pray thou, this desire thou, that thou may be despoiled of all manner of self, and thou, bare, follow Jesus only and die to thyself and live everlastingly in me. Then shall end all vain fantasies, wicked conturbations and superfluous cares; then also shall go away inordinate dread and inordinate love shall die."

(*The scene darkens and closes.*)

HUGH. And now, as slap contrast, we move from a girl's bedroom in Ireland to a back-sitting-room in London, probably in one of those awful terraces near Paddington Station. It's late afternoon and there's a touch of fog outside and it's neither cold nor hot. There's a ghastly red wall-paper on the walls and imitation eighteenth-century prints—for we'd like to pretend we're Harley Street, but of course we're miles too far west. And a maid with a dirty apron has shown us in and here we are, poor old Aunt Moll and Sallie Long.

(*And there they are, in mackintoshes and hats, sitting opposite each other at the centre table.*)

AUNT MOLL. I don't like this place.

SALLIE. It's all right.

AUNT MOLL. What is he like, this doctor of yours?

SALLIE. All right.

AUNT MOLL. I don't believe you.

SALLIE. Well, of course, he couldn't be quite all right to be what he is and to do what he's prepared to do.

AUNT MOLL. Hm. (SALLIE *shivers and catches her breath in a sob*.) Sallie, come away, come out of this place, it's evil.

SALLIE. No. I'm going through with it.

AUNT MOLL. Have courage. Think of Bernard Shaw.

SALLIE. It's pretty easy for him. He never had to bear an illegitimate baby; he need only talk light-heartedly about them.

AUNT MOLL. Child, I'll do anything I can to help you.

SALLIE. Dear Aunt Moll, you've done so much coming with me to London like this—don't leave me now. Call me a little coward if you like. I am, but I couldn't face mother; she's fond of me, she'd forgive me like a shot, but she'd be so sorry, so terribly sorry: and father—he wouldn't be cross, but he'd be so hurt and sorry. Oh, I couldn't bear people being sorry for me!

AUNT MOLL. I know. But don't let them be sorry. Be proud, be gay.

SALLIE. You're talking out of your reading, Aunt Moll, not out of common sense. There's nothing proud or gay in having an unwanted fatherless baby. And I'm not going to do it, I'm not going to do it. (*Getting more and more hysterical*.) Go on, walk out of here, don't get yourself mixed up in anything dirty and questionable. I thought you were my friend, the only real friend I had in Knock, but you're as conventional as the rest. Go back by the train to-night, eight forty-five from Euston, isn't it? Tell in Knock to-morrow afternoon where you saw me last, in a questionable doctor's waiting-room near Paddington. Tell them all I was going to do, have done to me, tell Jim's parents——

AUNT MOLL. You're talking nonsense. Pull yourself together. You know I'm your friend.

SALLIE. I'm sorry, Aunt Moll, I'm sorry.

(DOCTOR SMITH *comes in, a greasy, plausible man.*)

DOCTOR SMITH (*to* SALLIE). Good afternoon, Mrs. Smith.

SALLIE. Good afternoon, Doctor Smith. This is my aunt, Miss—Miss——

AUNT MOLL. Smith.

DOCTOR SMITH. Good afternoon, Miss Smith. We talked the matter over very fully the last time you were here, Mrs. Smith.

SALLIE. Yes, we did. I have the money here. (*She opens her bag.*)

DOCTOR SMITH. In notes?

SALLIE. In notes. (*She counts them out.*)

DOCTOR SMITH. I'll ring for Nurse Smith. (*He does so.*)

AUNT MOLL. Is everyone here called Smith?

DOCTOR SMITH. It is a convenient name, Miss—er—Smith. (*Taking the notes.*) Thank you.

SALLIE. You haven't counted them.

DOCTOR SMITH. I am sure that will not be necessary. I know a lady when I meet one.

AUNT MOLL. How long will it—I mean, how long, I mean——

DOCTOR SMITH. Oh, a short time, a very short time.

AUNT MOLL. I mean, how soon will my niece be out and about?

DOCTOR SMITH. Oh, a short time, a very short time. Ah, here is Nurse Smith.

> (NURSE SMITH, *not too smart a nurse, appears.*)

DOCTOR SMITH. Miss Smith, will you take Mrs. Smith downstairs. I shall follow you in a few minutes.

> (NURSE SMITH *makes* SALLIE *get up and come with her. As she passes to go out* AUNT MOLL *goes to her.*)

AUNT MOLL. My darling child.

SALLIE. If anything happens, tell Jim that —no, better tell him nothing.

> (*She goes out.*)

DOCTOR SMITH. Nothing bad can possibly happen, Miss Smith. As I said, in a short time, a very short time——

> (*The scene suddenly goes black. The platform at the back on which the bench*

*was is illuminated as a surpliced clergy-*
*man appears.)*

CLERGYMAN. I am the resurrection and the life, saith the Lord, and whoso liveth and believeth in Me shall never die. For the trumpet shall sound and the dead shall be raised incorruptible and we shall be changed. . . . For as much as it hath pleased Almighty God to take unto himself the soul of our dear sister here departed, we therefore commit her body to the ground; earth to earth, ashes to ashes, dust to dust.

*(His voice fades away and scene darkens.)*
*(A light comes up.* JIM DALY *is sitting by the fire writing on a pad on his knee.)*

JIM DALY. Darling Mums—I have got my final with flying colours and apparently a medal thrown in, gold they tell me, but I expect brass or maybe leather. Anyhow I've made up my mind to take a special course, so I won't be able to get home before the summer. Any news of Sallie? She hasn't answered my last two letters. The weather here is pretty good. I'm going to a Rugger dance at the Metropole to-night and on Thursday I'm going——

*(The scene fades. We see* HUGH *and* AUNT MOLL; *she is without mackintosh and hat, she seems to be crying.)*

HUGH. What *is* the matter, Aunt Moll?

AUNT MOLL. I'm foolish, I suppose, but it seemed so real.

HUGH. Nonsense. It's all in my mind. A figment of the imagination, as they say.

AUNT MOLL. Is it? Are you sure?

HUGH. Certain. I'm not a story-teller for nothing. Ssh! I hear them getting up inside; they'll be in in a minute. I'll prove to you it's all fancy. I'll ask Miss Pettigrew to show me what's in her bag, she'll let me search it; there'll be no sausage-rolls there and that will prove to you how imaginary the whole thing is.

AUNT MOLL. Please God.

*(The door from the dining-room opens, everyone comes in as they went in at the beginning of the play.)*

JIM. Whew! I've eaten too much, Mrs. Riordan.

JACK. Same here. You certainly gave us a meal to-night, Mother.

MISS PETTIGREW. Quite a collation, Mrs. Riordan. Wasn't it, Lucy?

MRS. DE LACY. Sumptuous.

MRS. RIORDAN. Well, indeed, I'm glad you liked it, but I think you hardly took a pick.

SALLIE. Indeed no.

MR. RIORDAN. I think we've all done remarkably well, Mother, except Hugh. And you were the belle of the ball, Hugh, and you only looked in for a minute to get a glass of milk for Aunt Moll.

HUGH. Oh, I stole a glass of claret for myself, Daddy.

MR. RIORDAN. Claret?　Sure that's no drink for a man.

MISS PETTIGREW (*coyly*). We missed you, Mr. Hugh.

HUGH. I'm sorry.　I was talking to Aunt Moll.

MRS. RIORDAN. Oh, did you get your milk, Aunt Moll?　I forgot about it.

AUNT MOLL. Oh yes, Aunt Moll got her milk.　She took care she got her milk; she saw to it herself.

HUGH. You mean I got it for you.

MR. RIORDAN. I think we might have a game or a song or something. How soon will the table be cleared, Kate?　Can't we play ping-pong?

MRS. RIORDAN. You must give Maggie ten minutes.

JIM. After that supper?　Have a heart, Mr. Riordan.

MRS. RIORDAN. I thought later on we might clear the floor and have a bit of a dance.

JIM. Fine.

MOLLIE. I'm not allowed to dance.

MRS. RIORDAN. Of course not, dear.

MR. RIORDAN. Then let's have a song.　I'm in the humour for a bit of music.　After all, I nearly won the Captain's prize.

MRS. RIORDAN. Yes, I think a little music would be nice.　Would you like some music, Mrs. de Lacy?

MRS. DE LACY. As long as it's not jazz.

MISS PETTIGREW. Oh, I love jazz. Of course I can't dance it. (*She laughs sillily.*)

MRS. RIORDAN. Honor, will you——?

HONOR. A terrible cold. Really, truly, Mrs. Riordan, not just an excuse.

MRS. RIORDAN. Isn't that too bad. Miss Long?

SALLIE LONG. I only sing when mother wants the room cleared.

JIM. Oh, nonsense, Sallie.

SALLIE. No, quite imposs. (*Turning to* JACK) But, Mr. Jack?

JACK. Nothing doing.

MISS PETTIGREW. But you sing most beautifully.

JACK. Never had a lesson in my life.

MISS PETTIGREW. Like the nightingales—not that I've ever heard one; there are none in Ireland I believe, quite extraordinary.

JIM. Come on, Jack. Give us a rouser.

MR. RIORDAN. Yes, start it rolling, Jack, something lively. Hugh, put a freshener in that, will you?

(*He hands him his glass.* HUGH *goes into the dining-room with it.*)

MRS. RIORDAN. Yes, do, dear. Mollie will play your accompaniment, won't she?

JACK. I should rather think she will. That's the reason why I married her.

MOLLIE. The only reason?

JACK. No, not the only reason. Come on, let's get it over.

AUNT MOLL. The song I asked you for, Jack.

JACK. "So, we'll go no more a-roving"? All right.

MISS PETTIGREW. Now I think this is going to be delightful. We hear so little music in Knock nowadays. I remember long ago what a lot of music there used to be at little parties like this. Do you remember, Lucy, how you and I used to sing that duet "Oh, that we two were maying"? And you were magnificent, Lucy, in "When sparrows build".

MRS. DE LACY. Hush.

MISS PETTIGREW. These gramophones and wireless have killed all real music, that's what I always say. Give me the good amateur every time, every time, every——

HONOR. A cushion behind you, Miss Pettigrew?

MISS PETTIGREW. Thank you, dear. Ah, they're beginning. How well Mollie plays.

MRS. DE LACY. Ssh!

MISS PETTIGREW. All right, my dear. I hope I know good music when I hear it.

    (MOLLIE *plays quite well.* JACK *sings well in an untrained voice.*)

JACK (*singing*).

    So, we'll go no more a-roving
      So late into the night,

Though the heart be still as loving,
　　And the moon be still as bright.

For the sword outwears its sheath,
　　And the soul wears out the breast,
And the heart must pause to breathe,
　　And even love have rest.

Though the night was made for loving,
　　And the day returns too soon,
Yet we'll go no more a-roving
　　By the light of the moon.

> (*The song captures the room.* MR. *and*
> MRS. RIORDAN *sit back vaguely pleased.*
> MR. RIORDAN'S *whiskey has been brought
> to him somewhere in the song by* HUGH,
> *who remains in the background.* MISS
> PETTIGREW *and her sister become senti-
> mental but not comically so.* JIM *is very
> quiet.* HONOR *is holding herself in
> stonily.* SALLIE *is on the verge of a
> break-down. No one could guess what*
> AUNT MOLL *thinks, she is very quiet.*
> HUGH *watches it all, takes it all in in
> growing excitement. The song stops,
> there is an instant of silence.*)

MRS. RIORDAN. Thank you, dear. How
well you play, Mollie.

> (*A little conventional murmur of thanks
> runs round the room.* SALLIE *gets up
> and crosses to the fire, swaying a little on
> her feet.*)

163

SALLIE. I can't—Jim——

HONOR (*at her side at once*). My dear, you're a little faint, aren't you? May we go into the hall, just for a minute, Mrs. Riordan?

MRS. RIORDAN. Of course. But——

> (*Almost before she can answer* HONOR *has got* SALLIE *out of the room.*)

MR. RIORDAN. What's happened? Is she ill?

AUNT MOLL. Not at all, Joseph. Don't be ridiculous.

MRS. RIORDAN. Just a touch of faintness.

MOLLIE. It *is* hot in here.

MISS PETTIGREW. Such a good supper.

HUGH (*who has got* JIM *aside; he talks to him with intensity, but in a low voice so that the others don't hear him*). She *is* ill and you know why. You know. Why don't you go to her? Why don't you?

JIM. I? I?——

HUGH (*almost shaking him*). Yes, you. You!

MISS PETTIGREW. It's such a pleasant party, Mrs. Riordan, one of the nicest I've been to this winter, but of course Mr. Hugh's being here makes all the difference.

HUGH (*turning from* JIM, *and now he affects a gaiety*). Yes, and now I'm going to have a joke on you all, at least I'm going to try a mild little joke on you, Miss Pettigrew. I want to search your bag.

MISS PETTIGREW. My bag?

HUGH. Yes. What have you got in your bag?

MISS PETTIGREW (*with a nervous, affected laugh*). Do you think I've taken some of your mother's silver forks?

HUGH. Of course not. But may I search it?

MISS PETTIGREW. Certainly not.

MRS. RIORDAN. What a crazy notion.

MR. RIORDAN. What's the idea, Hugh? Is it a game?

HUGH (*holding himself in, trying to speak lightly*). No, not exactly a game, Daddy, but all the future, all truth, all reality depends on the answer to my question. Aunt Moll, *you* know what I mean?

AUNT MOLL. I do.

(HONOR *and* SALLIE *come in.*)

HONOR. We're feeling quite all right, Mrs. Riordan. It was just your very good supper and your very hot fire.

MRS. RIORDAN. I think it's high time for a nice round game or some more music. Would you like that, Mrs. de Lacy?

MRS. DE LACY. Yes, indeed. Anything you choose.

HUGH (*wildly*). No, no. There are more important things going on in this room than a little music or a good round game. Miss Pettigrew, what's in your bag?

MRS. RIORDAN. Hugh, dear——

AUNT MOLL. As Mr. Shaw says, "Press your question, press your question."

HUGH. I won't, I can't, I couldn't bear to find it was true. Oh, have it your own way.

(*He goes out quickly.*)

MRS. RIORDAN. I'm sorry, he's so overtired. No sleep coming over and he has to go back to-morrow.

MISS PETTIGREW. To-morrow? So soon?

MRS. RIORDAN. Yes, some new play coming on, I think. Jack dear, turn on the wireless, there's sure to be a dance-band somewhere, and let's have a game of Slippery Sam. You might as well bring in the claret-cup and the sandwiches from the sideboard—and the decanter and siphon. Aunt Moll, are you going to play? (*But* AUNT MOLL *can't answer, she has her head in her hands.*) What's the matter? Aren't you well?

AUNT MOLL (*getting up and going to the door*). I'm a stupid old woman. Let me be, Kate. I'm going to Hugh.

(*She goes out.*)

MR. RIORDAN. Poor old Aunt Moll, she's beginning to break up. Give me the cards, Kate. I'll deal.

(*They pull their chairs round the table, talking and laughing, but before the game starts the curtain has fallen.*)

THE END

*December–March* 1933–34. DUBLIN–ARLES.

*Printed in Great Britain by* R. & R. CLARK, LIMITED, *Edinburgh.*